TANYA RONDER

Tanya Ronder trained at RADA and worked as an actress before turning to writing. Her other plays include *Peribanez* by Lope de Vega and *Vernon God Little* by DBC Pierre, nominated for an Olivier Award for Best New Play (Young Vic); *Blood Wedding* and *Filumena* by Eduardo de Filippo (Almeida); Ionesco's *Macbett* (RSC); *Table* and Pirandello's *Liolà* (National Theatre); *Peter Pan* (Kensington Gardens, the O2 and USA tour); *Night Flight* (Muztheater, Amsterdam) and *The Blake Diptych* (Fleur Darkin Ensemble).

Her work for film includes *King Bastard*.

Tanya Ronder

TABLE

NICK HERN BOOKS

London

www.nickhernbooks.co.uk

A Nick Hern Book

Table first published in Great Britain as a paperback original in 2013 by Nick Hern Books Limited, The Glasshouse, 49a Goldhawk Road, London W12 8QP

Table copyright © 2013 Tanya Ronder

Tanya Ronder has asserted her right to be identified as the author of this work

Cover image by Charlotte Wilkinson
Cover design by Ned Hoste, 2H

Typeset by Nick Hern Books, London
Printed and bound in Great Britain by CPI Group (UK) Ltd

A CIP catalogue record for this book is available from the British Library

ISBN 978 1 84842 328 2

Author's Note

This play was developed with the support of the National Theatre Studio, evolving through workshops with director Rufus Norris. The following actors took part in the workshops: Naana Agyei-Ampadu, Jamie Ballard, Clare Burt, Daniel Cerqueira, Chipo Chung, Rosalie Craig, Jonathan Cullen, Joseph Drake, Katie Fleetwood, Ian Gelder, Harry Hadden-Paton, Paul Hilton, Kobna Holdbrook-Smith, Jenny Jules, Rory Kinnear, Martina Laird, Penny Layden, Lyndsey Marshal, Andrew Maud, Itxaso Moreno, Sarah Niles, Lauren O'Neil, Matthew Pidgeon, Jessica Raine, Maggie Service, Michael Shaeffer, Sharon Small, Rebecca Sutherland and Sophie Wu. *Table* is full of moments inspired by the above.

The following script was created for the first production of *Table,* which opened The Shed at the National Theatre in April 2013. Some of the stage directions reflect the set created for that space, where the table was mounted on a large, low platform, surrounded by audience on three sides. At the back there was another long, thin platform, with chairs. This enabled us to use different playing areas at the same time, allowing 'ghosting' of different time-frames, or the resonance of an ancestor passing through, or simply providing an off-stage space. Another production can, of course, find different solutions. Likewise, the hymns and music noted are the choices used for this production, they're not imperatives.

Tanya Ronder

National Theatre

THE SHED

Table had its premiere in April 2013 as the first play to be staged in The Shed: a temporary venue created during the refurbishment of the National Theatre's studio theatre, to celebrate new theatre that is original, ambitious and unexpected.

The NT is central to the creative life of the UK. In its three theatres on the South Bank in London it presents an eclectic mix of new plays and classics from the world repertoire, with seven or eight productions in repertory at any one time. And through an extensive programme of amplifying activities – Platform performances, backstage tours, publications, and exhibitions – it recognises that theatre doesn't begin and end with the rise and fall of the curtain. The National endeavours to maintain and re-energise the great traditions of the British stage and to expand the horizons of audiences and artists alike. It aspires to reflect in its repertoire the diversity of the nation's culture. It takes a particular responsibility for the creation of new work – offering at the NT Studio a space for research and development for the NT's stages and the theatre as a whole. Through its Learning programme, it invites people of all ages to discover the NT's repertoire, the skills and excitement of theatre-making, and the building itself. As the national theatre, it aims to foster the health of the wider British theatre through policies of collaboration and touring. Between 20 and 26 new productions are staged each year in one of the NT's three theatres. In 2012–13, the National's total reach was over three million people worldwide, through attendances on the South Bank, in the West End, on tour and through National Theatre Live, the digital broadcast of live performances to cinema screens all over the world.

Information: +44 (0)20 7452 3400
Box Office: +44 (0)20 7452 3000
National Theatre, South Bank, London SE1 9PX
www.nationaltheatre.org.uk
Registered Charity No: 224223

Table was first performed in The Shed at the National Theatre, London, on 12 April 2013 (previews from 9 April), with the following cast:

ALBERT/ORION	Daniel Cerqueira
ELIZABETH/SARAH	Rosalie Craig
FINLEY/ANTHONY/CHRIS	Jonathan Cullen
JACK/GIDEON	Paul Hilton
MOTHER SUPERIOR/ MICHELLE/BARBARA	Penny Layden
SISTER HOPE/STACEY/VERONIQUE	Sarah Niles
MARGARET/SISTER BABETTE/ AISHA	Maggie Service
DAVID/JULIAN	Michael Shaeffer
SISTER RUTH/SU-LIN/JESS	Sophie Wu

Director	Rufus Norris
Designer	Katrina Lindsay
Lighting Designer	Paule Constable
Movement Director	Javier De Frutos
Music	David Shrubsole
Sound Designer	Rich Walsh

A Family Tree

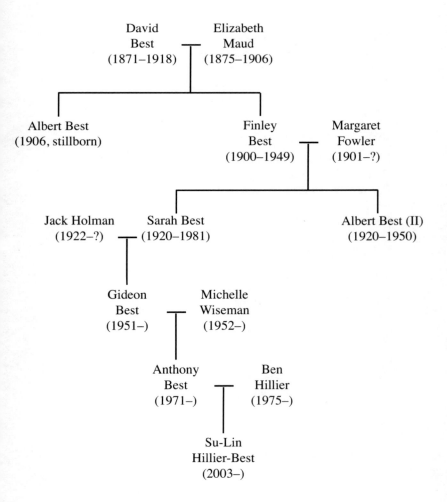

David Best (1871–1918) — Elizabeth Maud (1875–1906)

Albert Best (1906, stillborn)

Finley Best (1900–1949) — Margaret Fowler (1901–?)

Jack Holman (1922–?) — Sarah Best (1920–1981)

Albert Best (II) (1920–1950)

Gideon Best (1951–) — Michelle Wiseman (1952–)

Anthony Best (1971–) — Ben Hillier (1975–)

Su-Lin Hillier-Best (2003–)

Characters and Settings

LICHFIELD, STAFFORDSHIRE, 1898–1946

DAVID BEST
ELIZABETH, *David's wife*
FINLEY, *David and Elizabeth's son*
MARGARET FOWLER, *Finley's neighbour / wife*
ALBERT (II), *Finley and Margaret's son (twin)*
SARAH, *Finley and Margaret's daughter (twin)*
VERONIQUE

TANGANYIKA, AFRICA, 1950–1957

SARAH, *already listed above*
HOPE, *a nun*
BABETTE, *a nun*
RUTH, *a nun*
MOTHER SUPERIOR
JACK HOLMAN, *big-cat hunter*
GIDEON, *Sarah's son*

HEREFORDSHIRE, 1964–1981

SARAH, *already listed above*
GIDEON, *already listed above*
JACK, *already listed above*
JULIAN, *founder member of commune*
ORION, *founder member of commune*
STACEY, *founder member of commune*
AISHA, *daughter of commune*
BARBARA, *daughter of commune*
CHRIS, *commune member*
JESS, *commune member*
MICHELLE WISEMAN, *Gideon's wife*
ANTHONY, *Gideon and Michelle's son*

SOUTH LONDON, 2013

MICHELLE, *already listed*
ANTHONY, *already listed*
GIDEON, *already listed*
SU-LIN, *Anthony's daughter*

Note on Text

A forward slash (/) in the text indicates where the next character starts speaking, overlapping current speech.

The story takes place in four time frames: Lichfield 1898–1946, Tanganyika 1950–1957, Herefordshire 1964–1981 and South London 2013.

At the National Theatre, we used a cast of nine, but the cast size could be different in another production.

Acknowledgements

Thank you to Lucian Msamati for his Swahili translations and song, and to Tom Bompa Harding for 'Oh Jemima, where's your Uncle Jim…'

T.R.

This text went to press before the end of rehearsals and so may differ slightly from the play as performed.

FIRST HALF

Part One

A room with a substantial wooden table in it. London, 2013.
SU-LIN (*nine*) *and* GIDEON (*sixty-one*) *stand and look at it
from afar.*

SU-LIN. I hate this table, or should I not say that?

GIDEON. It's yours, you can say what you like.

SU-LIN. It's not mine.

GIDEON. It will be.

SU-LIN. I don't want it. I'm going to buy a big glass one from
Ikea.

GIDEON. What'll you do with this?

SU-LIN. Freecycle? It's mank.

GIDEON. Why?

SU-LIN. Look at it, it's all cacked-up.

GIDEON. What's cacked it up, though?

SU-LIN. What do you mean?

GIDEON. Pick a cack-up, any cack-up.

SU-LIN. What?

GIDEON. Want to see a coffin scratch?

SU-LIN. Is that the big one?

GIDEON. It's not, no, nobody knows how that one happened.

SU-LIN. That one, then?

She points. He shakes his head.

GIDEON. Leopard claws.

SU-LIN. Not true.

GIDEON. True.

SU-LIN. What's that from?

GIDEON. Mad nun's nails.

SU-LIN. That pale bit?

GIDEON. Bleach. Or possibly urine.

SU-LIN. Urgh.

She indicates a new patch.

That?

GIDEON. Heartburn.

SU-LIN. Those?

GIDEON. That's a thump, and that's a joke gone wrong.

SU-LIN. That?

DAVID (*twenty-six*) *appears in a woodworker's apron.*

GIDEON. Bits of flour from five thousand loaves of bread.

SU-LIN. That?

GIDEON. What, the sparkly bits?

SU-LIN. Which sparkly bits?

GIDEON. Tiny shards from twenty-seven million boring
 conversations.

SU-LIN. This?

GIDEON. Prayers.

SU-LIN. Prayers?

SU-LIN *moves off. Lichfield, 1898.* DAVID, *a perfectionist,
inspects the table with his thumb and fingers, ensuring every
inch is entirely smooth. He is mirrored by* GIDEON.
GIDEON *slides underneath the table, touching it from
beneath. He sings to himself.*

GIDEON (*singing*).
>   Dear Lord and Father of Mankind
>   Forgive our foolish ways
>   Re-clothe us in our rightful mind
>   In purer lives thy service find
>   In deeper reverence praise
>   In deeper reverence praise.

DAVID takes off his apron, puts it away. He attaches a buttonhole to his dark jacket. A door opens. There is a spill of light.

ELIZABETH. Hello, husband.

DAVID turns to see his bride. He goes to pick her up.

DAVID. Hello, missus. Welcome home.

He carries her in.

ELIZABETH (*seeing the table*). What's that doing out the workshop?

DAVID. It's for us.

ELIZABETH. Oh, David!

She exhales.

DAVID (*with some pride*). Well, it's solid.

ELIZABETH. For whoever ends up sitting at it. Eating, spilling gravy, doing schoolwork at it, God bless us all.

They admire it together. DAVID adores her, but is less comfortable with romance than work.

What now?

DAVID. An early night, perhaps…?

ELIZABETH (*shy*). Do you think?

She smiles, heads for the stairs. He lays her veil on the table. A tiny rough spot catches DAVID's attention.

Hey.

DAVID (*caught out*). Mm?

ELIZABETH. Are you spending your wedding night down here with your table?

DAVID. No, Mrs Best, I'm not.

They leave. London, 2013. SU-LIN (*nine*) *sits on the table wearing* ELIZABETH*'s veil and some headphones, singing a Chinese pop song* (*music by David Shrubsole, lyrics by Huan Wang*).

SU-LIN (*singing*). *U go mo yam zan tzoy foo gno sang… (Etc.)*

MICHELLE (*sixty*), *comes in with a mop.* ANTHONY (*forty-one*), *distracted, from off.*

ANTHONY (*off*). Right.

MICHELLE. Are you off?

ANTHONY (*off*). Yep.

MICHELLE. Right.

ANTHONY (*off*). Su-Lin, make sure you help Granny-'Chelle, won't you?

SU-LIN (*singing*). *Mo soh why men ya gno hay tzoy wa… (Etc.)*

ANTHONY (*off*). Right, see you later, Mum.

MICHELLE. Got everything?

ANTHONY (*off*). Mmm.

MICHELLE. Car keys?

He's so tense he could burst. He checks pockets, rushes in.

ANTHONY. No, my keys, what did I do with my stupid keys?

MICHELLE. Anthony, calm down.

ANTHONY (*to* SU-LIN). Sorry, love, you haven't seen the car keys, have you?

SU-LIN (*singing*). *Ho bi tzoi mun soy hey gno… (Etc.)*

ANTHONY. I put them somewhere. Why am I so rubbish?

MICHELLE. When did you last have them?

ANTHONY. Coming back from shopping.

SU-LIN finds them. She speaks in made-up Chinese.

SU-LIN. *Tsing cha. (Etc.)*

ANTHONY. Perfect, thank you, love, all set.

SU-LIN responds in her Chinese persona. MICHELLE and ANTHONY have a moment.

MICHELLE. Alright?

ANTHONY. Mmn. Hot.

She helps him take off his coat.

MICHELLE. He's not Superman.

ANTHONY breathes out.

Better?

ANTHONY. Sorry. Sorry, Mum.

MICHELLE. And you're not rubbish, you just have high expectations.

He goes.

Look at the state of this floor, Su-Lin.

SU-LIN takes off her headphones.

SU-LIN. *Yo-sa-me.*

MICHELLE. Translate.

SU-LIN (*Chinese accent*). Hello, I am your Chinese maid.

MICHELLE. I expect a top job, then, if you're a trained maid and all.

SU-LIN (*Chinese accent*). Very professional, ten years old –

MICHELLE. Nine. Where d'you get the veil from?

SU-LIN (*her natural London accent*). Dressing up. It smells of dust.

She watches MICHELLE *mop*.

Are you angry?

MICHELLE. No.

SU-LIN. Sad?

MICHELLE. No.

SU-LIN. Can I have another Easter egg?

MICHELLE. After dinner.

SU-LIN. I don't think I'm going to have dinner today.

MICHELLE. You are gonna have dinner, we've got guests.

SU-LIN. Guest. Is that why you're angry?

MICHELLE. I'm not angry! I'm not, sweetheart, honest, I'm just concentrating, there's lots to do.

SU-LIN. What's so scary about Grandpa?

Beat.

MICHELLE. Who told you you should call him Grandpa?

SU-LIN. He is my grandpa.

MICHELLE. But you've never met him.

SU-LIN. Doesn't make him not my grandpa. I like your top, you look pretty.

MICHELLE. Thank you, so do you.

SU-LIN. Dada-Ben said I should wear it.

MICHELLE. Pop the veil upstairs, now, and come and help.

SU-LIN. I like it.

MICHELLE. It's not ideal to clean in, though, is it?

SU-LIN. When did you last see him?

MICHELLE. A lifetime ago.

SU-LIN. Umm! Why?

MICHELLE. He's been busy.

SU-LIN. Busy how?

MICHELLE. Making cement.

SU-LIN. Cement? That sounds heavy.

MICHELLE *laughs*.

MICHELLE. He doesn't carry it with him. He travels, helps communities make mortar, which is basically cement or like strong glue.

SU-LIN. To build their houses with?

MICHELLE. Yep.

SU-LIN. That's a weird career.

MICHELLE. Yep. We used to have a lime-kiln out the back of the house. He did want to be an architect.

SU-LIN. Like you?

MICHELLE. Mmm, but ended up careering slightly off his career.

SU-LIN. What's careering?

MICHELLE. Like a car crash.

SU-LIN. Will you recognise him?

MICHELLE. Oh, God, I expect so.

Under the table, GIDEON *turns*.

SU-LIN. He won't recognise me cos he's never seen me.

MICHELLE. No.

SU-LIN *follows* MICHELLE *off*. GIDEON *starts humming. Encouraged by* ELIZABETH (*pregnant*) *and* DAVID (*thirty-four*), *young* FINLEY (*six*) *comes on singing the song* GIDEON *hums. Music by Gounod – the 'Soldiers' Chorus' from* Faust, *words traditional*.

FINLEY (*singing*).

> Oh Jemima, where's your Uncle Jim?
> He's under the water, teaching the ducks to swim.

They all do the hand gestures, paddling like swimming ducks, etc.

> First he does the breaststroke, then he does the side,
> And now he's under the water, swimming against the tide.

They're easy and familial.

> Oh don't be unkind to a duck (quack quack),
> For a duck may be somebody's *mo*ther,
> They always live in the swamp,
> Where the weather is always domp.
> Now you may think that this is the end,
> Well it is.

ELIZABETH *leaves.* FINLEY *watches her go.* DAVID *gets a pot.*

DAVID. Mrs Fowler brought this round. Lamb stew.

FINLEY. Why didn't the baby have a coffin?

DAVID. It was too small. She wouldn't have wanted it to be on its own.

FINLEY. She's left me on my own.

DAVID. No she's not, Fin. Run and fetch a mat, will you, we'll have a spot of stew.

FINLEY. Was it a girl, in the end?

DAVID. A boy.

FINLEY. We can't call him Florence then.

DAVID. No.

FINLEY. Would she still be alive if she'd had a girl?

DAVID. No.

FINLEY. We'd know what the baby was called, though.

DAVID. I need a mat, Fin, the pan's scalding.

FINLEY. His name's Albert, baby Albert.

DAVID. Where do you get that from?

FINLEY. He told me, that's his name. Show me what you were making. When she shouted for you and you didn't come, what were you working on, a table?

DAVID. A cupboard.

FINLEY. For us?

DAVID. For Mrs Brook.

FINLEY. Who's Mrs Brook?

DAVID. A lady, she lives at the Lodge. Take this.

> *Beat.*

It's not her fault, Fin, she's / a customer.

FINLEY. A customer.

DAVID (*sharply*). Take the pan, Finley.

> FINLEY *takes it.*

Don't touch the sides, just the handles, got it?

> DAVID *heads off.* FINLEY *stands with the pot. He puts it down on the table.* DAVID *returns with a mat. Nervous,* FINLEY *retrieves the pan.* DAVID *leaps to rub the mark off with his tea towel. It is burnt.*

FINLEY. Sorry, Pa, sorry.

DAVID. Sorry? What kind of an excuse is sorry? I didn't mean that, Fin.

FINLEY. You did.

DAVID. Finley, lad, the door to the workshop was shut, I couldn't hear, I didn't hear her call.

FINLEY. Or you were too busy making your furniture.

> SU-LIN *calls from off.*

SU-LIN (*off*). Granny-'Chelle?

MICHELLE (*off*). You okay?

SU-LIN (*off*). Where are you?

MICHELLE (*off*). Kitchen. I'm just about to light the oven, do you want to do the ignition?

SU-LIN (*off*). Okay. *Tsa tsa tzoo…* (*Etc.*)

MICHELLE (*off*). *Tsa tsa tzoo*, yourself.

> DAVID *puts his apron back on.* FINLEY *leaves. He whistles 'He Who Would Valiant Be' as he ages and changes into a First World War infantry jacket.* GIDEON *joins the whistling, he emerges from under the table.* FINLEY (*now sixteen*) *returns and takes out an infantry cap as* DAVID *takes out a sharpening stone.* FINLEY *puts on his cap, looks to* DAVID *for approval.* DAVID *can't meet his eye.*

DAVID. You don't have to go, Finley.

FINLEY. I know I don't. Father?

> *Silence.*

> FINLEY *leaves.* GIDEON *is lost in his own thoughts.* DAVID *takes his chisel and stabs it into the table, gouging the wood deeply.*

MARGARET (*off*). Lamb stew? Mother made extra…

> DAVID *climbs onto the table, lies face-up.* FINLEY (*eighteen*) *is back, with a bowl of water. His hand is bandaged. When he hears* MARGARET, *he tries to hide the bowl.* MARGARET (*eighteen*) *comes in.*

When are they collecting?

FINLEY. First thing.

MARGARET. Are you… you don't have to wash him, do you? They'll do that.

> *Beat.*

> FINLEY *wants private time with his father.*

Should I pop this in the kitchen? It's quite warm, but I can heat it through if you like it piping.

FINLEY. I'm not hungry.

She takes it to the kitchen. FINLEY, *defeated, puts the water down.* MARGARET *returns.*

MARGARET. He thought you'd never make it back. I bet you've seen some sights. The whole town knitted long johns for you, well, the girls did. Was it freezing?

FINLEY. Mm.

MARGARET. I hope some of them reached you.

FINLEY. I don't know if they were knitted by you.

He waits for her to go.

MARGARET. If you did want to wash him, I could help, I've done my first-aid course. Must be awkward with your hand. Shall I...?

She gets stuck in, undressing DAVID. FINLEY, *usurped, watches.*

Do you have fresh clothes?

FINLEY. Do I smell that bad?

She doesn't get the joke.

His suit's hanging on the mirror, upstairs.

MARGARET. He had it ready for your homecoming.

FINLEY. And here I am, home.

MARGARET. Thank the Merciful Lord. Did you get the toffees Mother sent?

FINLEY. Thank you, yes, they were popular.

MARGARET. I'll tell her. What will you do, will you take over the workshop?

He harrumphs.

What else can you do?

FINLEY. Good question.

MARGARET. There's plenty demand for packing-crates.

He sneers. She manhandles DAVID*'s body, gets his arms out his shirt.*

FINLEY. Impressively red cross.

MARGARET. I was hoping to complete the training.

FINLEY. Shame the war ended.

MARGARET. I didn't mean that. Don't you need more suds in there?

FINLEY. Don't know, you didn't get washed in France when you kicked it.

MARGARET. I would have said so, for a proper clean.

FINLEY. Voilà, another excuse of a job.

She starts to wash DAVID.

MARGARET. What were the nurses like, were they pretty?

FINLEY. Like all girls, some were.

MARGARET. That's what they're famous for – how pretty they are, and the amount of kisses they hand out, was that your experience?

FINLEY. What?

MARGARET. That the nurses were kissers.

FINLEY. Not the nurses.

MARGARET. Other girls, or, *an*other mademoiselle…?

FINLEY. Not kisses.

MARGARET. Oh.

She finishes washing between DAVID*'s fingers.*

I'm sorry about your father. 'His willing arms need work no more.'

FINLEY *addresses her openly for the first time.*

FINLEY. Where's that from?

MARGARET. One of the gravestones at the back of the churchyard.

FINLEY. I like it. It fits him.

She presses her advantage.

MARGARET. I'll fetch his suit.

FINLEY. The room with the double bed.

MARGARET. Did you mean that you had sex with prostitutes?

FINLEY. Does that disgust you?

MARGARET. It doesn't intimidate me, if that's what you're asking.

FINLEY. Well, neighbour, you're determined. You should see what some cunt-struck buggers came back with, rods like dead babies.

MARGARET. How could they?

He grabs her and ruts her fiercely, then, just as quickly, moves off. She recovers herself.

Do you have syphilis, Finley?

FINLEY. No.

MARGARET. Are you sure?

FINLEY. Want to look?

MARGARET. No.

FINLEY. I'll tell you, then, my dick's perfect, but I cannot vouch for anything else. I am crawling with uselessness.

MARGARET. You don't frighten me, Finley Best, although I think you'd like to. (*Kind but firm.*) You've been to war, young man, that's all.

They leave. Young ALBERT (eight) creeps on wearing a gas mask.

ALBERT (*singing*).
> Oh Jemima, where's your Uncle Jim?
> He's under the water, teaching the ducks to swim… (*Etc.*)

DAVID leaves. The gas lights are exchanged for electric.
SARAH (eight) whispers to ALBERT.

SARAH. Albert, I can't hear anything you're saying…

(*Meaning the mask.*) Take it off. I don't like it.

She runs on, tries to pull his mask off.

Take it off or I'll scream!

ALBERT whips off his mask, whispers to SARAH.

ALBERT. If you scream, you'll wake the baby.

SARAH. Which baby?

ALBERT. He's under the table.

ALBERT knocks on it without SARAH seeing.

It's the baby knocking.

SARAH. What for?

ALBERT. Ask him.

SARAH. No.

ALBERT. He wants to speak to you.

He knocks again.

SARAH. That's you, Albert!

ALBERT. It's not me, it's the other one, baby Albert.

SARAH. No it's not!

ALBERT. Do you know why baby Albert's stuck in the house?

SARAH. He's not stuck.

ALBERT. Because he carved his name, look.

He shows her under the table.

SARAH. 'A.B.'

ALBERT. Albert Best.

SARAH. Babies can't carve.

ALBERT. Who wrote it, then?

SARAH. Don't know.

ALBERT. He did.

MARGARET (*off*). It's not dinner time, yet.

FINLEY (*off*). I know.

MARGARET (*off*). Where are you going, then?

FINLEY (*off*). Knocking off.

SARAH *and* ALBERT *fall quiet*.

MARGARET (*off*). It's not voluntary work, Finley.

FINLEY (*off*). Do you think I'd be doing it if it was? Making crappy crates.

MARGARET (*off*). God doesn't care, so long as you provide.

FINLEY (*off*). No matter that it's killing me.

SARAH *nestles into* ALBERT.

MARGARET (*off*). Not exactly a hurried death, eight crates a day…

FINLEY (*off*). I can't do handstands either.

MARGARET (*off*). What do you want from me, Finley?

FINLEY (*off*). A fuck, maybe?

SARAH *sings to herself to block them out*. FINLEY *and* MARGARET *continue their argument*.

MARGARET (*off*). That's not an attractive thought right now.

FINLEY (*off*). Shall we make a date for later? When have you ever put yourself out, cushy Maggie?

MARGARET (*off*). Let's start with giving birth to twins, shall we?

FINLEY (*off*). Be thankful you didn't die in the process.

MARGARET (*off*). It would be nice to feel my husband was glad.

FINLEY (*off*). Gratitude is for cretins.

MARGARET (*off*). You're in a league of your own, too good for everything, yet you're the biggest slacker of the lot. Children, where are you? Time to lay the table!

   SARAH *and* ALBERT *stand alert.*

FINLEY (*off, taunting*). Kissy kissy…

MARGARET (*off*). Stop it!

FINLEY (*off*). What did I do? Tried to kiss my wife…

MARGARET (*off*). She doesn't want a kiss from you, it's the last thing on earth she wants!

   ALBERT *initiates a game, involving snogging the gas mask.*

FINLEY (*off*). I know, God damn it, I know!

MARGARET (*off*). 'No' is never enough, it never was.

FINLEY (*off, defensive*). My needs are my needs, what can I do?

MARGARET (*off*). You think I don't have needs? I'm bursting with them!

FINLEY (*off*). I'd like to feel you burst!

MARGARET (*off*). It's all you ever want, it's all you think about.

FINLEY (*off*). Well, at the end of the day, what else is there?

ALBERT. Let's play the game Daddy played with the dark lady, you come here.

SARAH. No, we'll get in trouble.

ALBERT. I'll be the dark lady, then, and they're making noises.

   He uses the table.

Aaaaarh, I am the bluebird... Come here and play, it's fun, it's really, really funny. 'Oooh, I am the bluebird and you are the bluebird!'

SARAH. 'I am the bluebird!'

SARAH *joins in, nervously, despite herself.*

ALBERT. Push, he's pushing her!

SARAH *laughs, pushes* ALBERT.

I'm a bluebird, I'm a bluebird.

SARAH *and* ALBERT. I am the bluebird – I am the bluebird... (*Etc.*)

MARGARET (*twenty-seven*) *comes in.*

MARGARET. What are you doing, what are you doing?

SARAH. Albert made me.

ALBERT *and* SARAH *stifle giggles.*

MARGARET (*to* ALBERT). What were you doing?

ALBERT. Animals, we were playing at animals.

MARGARET. What animals?

ALBERT. I was the bluebird and she was the bluebird.

ALBERT *gets a bout of nervous laughter.*

MARGARET. Why are you laughing – guilt, are you guilty?

SARAH. I wasn't the bluebird.

ALBERT. Sorry, Mummy.

SARAH. Sorry, Mummy, sorry, God.

MARGARET. What for?

SARAH. Being bad.

MARGARET. Bad, how?

ALBERT. Not laying the table.

SARAH. You have to tell the truth, Albert.

ALBERT. Shut up.

MARGARET. She won't, and you won't make her.

SARAH. I was Daddy and Albert was the dark lady.

ALBERT. Shut uuuup!

MARGARET. You look me in the eye and you tell me, Albert.

ALBERT. We were playing Daddy on top of the dark lady, pushing her.

MARGARET leaves, ALBERT and SARAH are frightened. She comes back with a belt and a bucket of water. SARAH kneels, praying.

MARGARET (*to* ALBERT). Mr know-it-all knows it all, does he, does he? Now, take that scrubbing brush and scrub, go on!

She indicates the place on the table where they were playing. ALBERT scrubs.

(*To* SARAH.) You must never let any man, ever, make you do that. Your brother, a man you love, a man who tells you he loves you, even your husband, it's not a game.

(*To* ALBERT.) Scrub the stains, dirty, filthy, useless…

She threatens the belt.

SARAH (*quietly*). / Dear God, we'll never play Daddy and the dark lady ever again, please don't hurt Albert… (*Etc.*)

MARGARET grabs the brush from ALBERT, uses it herself.

MARGARET. Scrub, scrub, scrub it out, scrub it clean, properly clean, clean it, clean it, clean it… (*Etc.*)

She forgets the children are there while she scrubs manically. SARAH sings quietly (traditional lyrics, music adapted by John Tams).

SARAH (*singing*).
      Lay me low, lay me low, lay me low
      Where no one can see me
      Where no one can find me
      Where no one can hurt me

GIDEON *joins the singing.*

SARAH *and* GIDEON (*singing*).
Show me the way, help me to say
All that I need to
All that I needed you gave me
All that I wanted you made me
When I stumbled you saved me
Lay me low…

MARGARET *prays.* VERONIQUE, *a prostitute, comes in, crooning 'I'm a Little Blackbird' (by George W Meyer and Arthur Johnston, lyrics by Roy Turk and Grant Clarke), with a woozy* FINLEY *in tow.*

FINLEY. Shhhh.

VERONIQUE *carries on singing.* GIDEON *sings too.* FINLEY *gets* VERONIQUE *on the edge of the table.*

VERONIQUE. Ooh, you're strong, Mr Finley, King Finley.

They are in the position ALBERT *reconstructed with* SARAH. ALBERT *watches, then backs away. Still singing,* VERONIQUE *pushes* FINLEY *into his chair. She straddles him.* FINLEY *climaxes quietly.*

FINLEY. Oh, Christ…

VERONIQUE *takes her money and leaves. An older* ALBERT (*thirteen*) *carries in a parcel. Very carefully, he unwraps* ELIZABETH's *wedding dress. He tries the dress against him, twirling the material, as if on a Parisian catwalk.* SARAH (*thirteen*) *finds him.*

SARAH. Albert?

ALBERT. Go to bed, Sarah.

SARAH. You'll get caught.

ALBERT. Go on, bugger off.

SARAH. Don't!

ALBERT. Bugger, bugger, bugger.

SARAH. Ask God's forgiveness.

ALBERT. What for, being brilliant?

SARAH. That's conceited.

ALBERT. Go away, Sarah.

SARAH. I won't.

ALBERT (*goading her*). Damn, blast, copulation, breasts, bowel, excrement –

SARAH (*praying*). Dear Father, please forgive Albert for the disgusting words he uses, he doesn't mean it, even though he knows how bad they are – (*Etc.*)

ALBERT. Vagina, anus, bastard, sod –

SARAH *comes back as strongly.*

SARAH. We will be restless until we rest in God.

ALBERT. When we bloody well die.

SARAH. No, now.

ALBERT. That explains why Mother's so peaceful, then. I hate them, I hate God, I hate you.

SARAH. How can you say that?

ALBERT. When you pray, God can't hear you because he's got no ears.

SARAH. Don't say things you don't know.

ALBERT. You just can't accept the truth.

SARAH *looks at him. He starts to wrap the dress back up.*

SARAH. Where did you find that?

ALBERT. Father's cupboard.

ALBERT *smoothes the dress on the table.*

When I leave home I'm going to go as far away as it's humanly possible to go.

SARAH. Where to?

ALBERT. I'm going to go to the Continent to learn about couture.

SARAH. What's 'couture'?

ALBERT. You'll see.

SARAH. We are twins, still. Are you coming to bed?

ALBERT. Not yet.

SARAH. Twins, except I don't hate you, at all.

> SARAH *and* ALBERT *set the table.* SARAH *serves.*
> FINLEY *stays seated.* GIDEON *voices the prayer with*
> MARGARET.

MARGARET. Dear Lord, we thank you for the meat on our plates, for the strength in our bodies, for the nourishment of our souls –

FINLEY. Arseholes.

MARGARET. – for the bounty laid before us –

FINLEY. I'll lay my bounty before you.

MARGARET, SARAH *and* ALBERT. Amen.

ALBERT. I've made a new friend.

MARGARET. Elbows off the table, Albert.

> *He takes them off.*

ALBERT. I've made a new friend.

MARGARET. What's his father's name?

ALBERT. She's called Catherine.

MARGARET. In your class?

ALBERT. She's just moved here, her father's a tailor.

MARGARET. Is that why you were late?

FINLEY. No dark meat today?

> *Beat.*

ALBERT. She says she's going to teach me how to sew.

MARGARET (*to* ALBERT). What are you talking about, Albert?

ALBERT. Why does nobody in this family understand what I say?

MARGARET. Not at table, Albert.

FINLEY. I prefer my meat dark.

Beat.

MARGARET. It's dinner time, not 'poor me' time. Self-pity rots you, Albert, inside and out. You don't see me going around feeling sorry for myself, do you?

ALBERT. All I said was I wanted to learn to sew.

FINLEY. Cross stitch? That's all women can teach.

FINLEY *tickles himself with this.* MARGARET *ignores him. To* ALBERT.

MARGARET. Well, you can't afford distraction, can you? How you're ever going to get to higher-grade school at this rate...

SARAH. He'll manage.

MARGARET. You've a different mindset, Sarah, it was easy for you. What is it you are wearing, Albert?

ALBERT. I was hot.

MARGARET. You are an embarrassment. There's cloth where your brains should be.

FINLEY. Delicious food, Mother, a proper mouthful.

SARAH. Please may I be excused from the table?

MARGARET. No.

Beat.

FINLEY. Does Catherine like a proper mouthful, Albert?

SARAH. I have Sunday school to prepare.

MARGARET. I said, no.

SARAH. And I've eaten enough.

MARGARET. Sit up, Albert, remember 'rot'. (*To* SARAH.)
You're not leaving this table, nobody is.

FINLEY. Nobody wants to, without pudding.

Beat.

Ripe plums for me.

ALBERT *stands.*

MARGARET. Where do you think you're going?

ALBERT. To the lavatory.

MARGARET. Sit down!

ALBERT. I need to go to the lavatory.

MARGARET. You're not leaving this table. What is wrong with
you, Albert? Sit down, I said sit!

ALBERT *unbuttons his fly, unfolds himself and urinates on
the table.*

What are you...?

Startled, they all move back from the splash.

Oh, dear God, stop it, stop!

He finishes.

ALBERT. You said nobody was to leave the table.

MARGARET. Sit in your chair.

ALBERT *sits.* SARAH *stands.*

(*To* SARAH.) Sit down, please. Join your family at the
dinner table.

FINLEY. A superior piece, made by superior hands.

MARGARET. Sit down. Sit down or I'll thrash the living
daylights out of you.

GIDEON *sings (traditional Christian/Spiritual).*

GIDEON (*singing*).
> There is a balm in Gilead,
> To make the wounded whole

SARAH *joins the singing.*

SARAH *and* GIDEON (*singing*).
> There is a balm in Gilead,
> To heal the sin-sick soul.

SARAH *is dressed in a nun's habit.* MARGARET *gets up,
clears table and leaves.* FINLEY *slumps in his chair.*

NUNS *and* SARAH (*singing*).
> Sometimes I feel discouraged
> And think my work's in vain,
> But then the Holy Spirit
> Revives my soul again.
>
> There is a balm in Gilead,
> To make the wounded whole
> There is a balm in Gilead,
> To heal the sin-sick soul.

Their song segues in to a traditional African song.

> Ah-way,
> Ah-way zaman gwa za.
> Ah-way,
> Ah-way zaman gwa za.
> Zaman gwa zaman yoh-way ah-way,
> Aman yoh-way
> Aman yoh-way.

*The table is wrapped up in blankets and sheets and tied with
rope.*

Part Two

The room in England disappears, the table is lifted into the air to the noise of a big ship in a busy port. Tanganyika, 1950. The NUNS *catch the table as it lowers into their hands.*

HOPE. Dear Lord God Almighty, thank You for carrying this treasure, which was once a tree from Your garden, Lord, or maybe two trees, or three, to Sarah. We are very grateful, and she, especially, is filled to the brim with thanks for its arrival, it's all she wanted from the house, although the reason for it coming, Lord, darkens her spirit, more than she will say, but I am sure You know, and are taking care of her brother's soul, despite everything. She will teach many people the holy word at this table, with Your blessing. Defend us today by Your mighty power, so that we may not fall into any sin, and that all our words may so proceed and all our thoughts and actions be so directed as to be always just in Your sight, through Christ our Lord, Amen.

They look at one another.

SARAH. I thought the boat would sink, or it would get abandoned in Rotterdam or something.

HOPE. Where was your faith, Sarah?

BABETTE. Shall we?

They start to untie the ropes. RUTH *reads the label.*

RUTH. 'Weight-bearing capacity – high.'

The NUNS *carefully unwrap the layers.*

BABETTE. How long since you saw it?

SARAH. Four years, when I last saw them.

HOPE. God rest their souls.

RUTH *starts*.

RUTH. What was that?

HOPE. What?

RUTH. There.

BABETTE. Spider.

HOPE. Spider?

BABETTE. Quite big.

She demonstrates, about an inch including legs.

RUTH. It fell off the green blanket.

She jumps onto the table. HOPE *and* BABETTE *gaze at the floor.*

BABETTE. There it is, kill it.

SARAH. We can't.

SARAH bends to look.

HOPE. Not with your hands, Sarah.

SARAH. I'm not. But it might be British, completely harmless.

RUTH. It couldn't travel all that way, could it?

SARAH inspects it.

HOPE. It could be a violin one.

BABETTE. Its legs aren't long enough, they're like daddy-long-legs.

RUTH. Or a huntsman. Did you see Betoto's foot last week? That was a huntsman.

BABETTE. Kill it.

SARAH. No, just leave it! I'll get the dustpan and brush.

HOPE. It's going to jump!

SARAH. It's not going to jump.

HOPE. Look.

BABETTE. Oh, I can't take this, we should just kill it!

SARAH. It's not attacking us.

She looks at it.

Huntsman ones are bigger.

HOPE. Don't trust it, just because it's little.

SARAH. I'm not.

HOPE. The jigger ones are the most deadly.

SARAH. They're parasites, not spiders.

BABETTE. Just get the equipment, Sarah.

SARAH. Well, I think it's British. Just leave my spider alone.

She goes.

BABETTE. Such a rigmarole, to preserve an insect's life.

HOPE *watches the spider closely. She suddenly leaps onto the table.* BABETTE *instinctively joins her.*

What?

HOPE. It jumped.

MOTHER SUPERIOR (*Irish, forties*) *enters.*

MOTHER SUPERIOR. What are you doing, sisters?

HOPE. I'm sorry, Mother Superior, a spider dropped from Sarah's table, and –

MOTHER SUPERIOR. Where?

HOPE. Down there.

MOTHER SUPERIOR *lifts her skirts to look.*

MOTHER SUPERIOR. What kind?

HOPE. We thought maybe a huntsman or a violin –

RUTH. Or a hobo…

HOPE. But then it jumped.

RUTH. Sarah's collecting the dustpan and brush.

BABETTE. There it is.

RUTH. It's climbing your leg.

HOPE. *Mungu utubariki*. [God bless us.]

MOTHER SUPERIOR. Lord, protect us.

SARAH comes back.

SARAH. Where's it gone?

BABETTE. There.

She points.

SARAH. Excuse me, Mother.

She sweeps the spider off her.

You'd think it was a crocodile.

BABETTE. No, because they stay in the lake.

SARAH. Look, I'm sure that's British, I don't know how it survived.

She offers up the dustpan. They fluster.

ALL. Don't drop him! – No! – Sarah!

SARAH (*to the spider*). Come on, to the yard with you, whoever you are.

BABETTE. Not far enough.

She goes.

MOTHER SUPERIOR. Good. Carry on unwrapping, sisters, then back to work.

HOPE. Thank you, Mother.

MOTHER SUPERIOR *sweeps off. The* NUNS *climb down. Cautiously, they continue to peel off the blankets.*

BABETTE. Open from the corners.

RUTH. My skin's crawling.

BABETTE. I squash them when I'm on my own.

When SARAH comes back, the table's dark, waxed wood is revealed; it takes her breath away. The SISTERS leave her to her privacy. SARAH is transfixed. She traces its scars, smells it, rubs her cheek on the wood.

SARAH. Hello, big scar. Mother. Father. Albert. I'm sorry I sailed without you.

ALBERT (twenty-six) speaks as if SARAH is there, though she is still at the convent, remembering.

ALBERT. But you're a guest and I'm used to it – let's not fight. I've got corned beef and I knew you'd want vegetables, there's potatoes and cabbage, coconut for pudding. We won it at the shy, didn't we, Daddy?

FINLEY. Nnng.

ALBERT. We won't wait. You're not wearing white. I thought dressing up was the main point of turning Catholic.

ALBERT spoon-feeds FINLEY (forty-six).

I can tell you're laughing. I'm surprised at you, Sarah, I thought you'd been working with people.

FINLEY biffs the spoon.

Stop it!

Slowly, SARAH takes her place at the table.

Daddy, will you please eat. Sarah thinks it's difficult, is it, Father?

SARAH. The house looks nice.

ALBERT. Thank you.

SARAH. The convent rooms are bare – floor, bed, that's it.

ALBERT. Lovely.

SARAH. I like the rug.

ALBERT. Thank you, I made it.

SARAH. Did you really?

ALBERT. Out of scraps.

SARAH. That's so clever, Albert.

ALBERT. I know.

SARAH. Is Mother –

ALBERT (*cutting her off*). Can we not talk about her now?

SARAH. Where is she?

ALBERT. Helping unfortunates.

> FINLEY *splashes his food.*

> Oh, God, stupid idiot, that's all down me!

SARAH. You shouldn't talk to him like that.

ALBERT. Don't tell me how to speak. You come in here and boss me around.

SARAH. What are you doing?

ALBERT. Clearing up.

SARAH. But we haven't started.

ALBERT. Tough nuts, you shouldn't have been bossy.

SARAH. Why don't you write back, Albert?

ALBERT. Why are you here?

SARAH. I... I was hoping everyone would –

ALBERT (*breaking her off*). What do you think, Daddy, should she just sod off?

SARAH. Albert, please.

ALBERT. What's wrong?

SARAH. You should have left! I never dreamt you'd stay.

ALBERT. Why? I have a spectacular life, I live in a nice house with a rag rug and Daddy for company. They didn't want me at war because I was necessary, classified as 'indispensable' at home, a lot more than can be said for you, where's your husband, where are your children? So, don't come here judging me.

FINLEY. Mmnng.

SARAH *knocks on the table*.

ALBERT. What do you do, pray to God and be kind to strangers?

SARAH. Knock knock.

ALBERT. Who's there?

SARAH. Albert.

ALBERT. Albert who?

SARAH. Baby Albert under the table.

Beat.

I've been invited to become a missionary nun.

ALBERT. Where?

SARAH. Tanganyika.

ALBERT. Oh. Why?

SARAH. People there need help.

ALBERT. And you want my opinion?

SARAH. If she's not back in time, please tell Mother I'd like to see her. If I do accept the place, I leave in November.

ALBERT. I won't see her before November.

SARAH. Why not?

ALBERT. She doesn't live here any more.

SARAH. What do you mean, where else does she live?

ALBERT. Who knows.

SARAH. Is this a joke?

ALBERT. Yes, ha, ha.

SARAH. What are you saying, Albert?

ALBERT. She left us.

SARAH. When?

ALBERT. After Father's turn.

SARAH. She can't do that! You're her family, she can't just leave...

ALBERT. Well, she did, so it looks like you're wrong, for once, ha, ha, ha again. Do you want some coconut, Daddy? Look, it's Sarah.

ALBERT *goes to the kitchen.* SARAH *is reeling from the news. She looks to* FINLEY *for some contact. He stretches his hand towards her, inappropriately. There's a bang from the kitchen as* ALBERT *breaks in to the coconut.* SARAH *flees.*

SARAH. I'll pray for you, Albert.

ALBERT *comes from the kitchen, sees she's not there.*

ALBERT. Did she leave? Has she gone, Father?

FINLEY. Mmmm.

ALBERT. Exactly, Daddy. Exactly.

SARAH *is back in her convent room, at her table.* HOPE *drills* SARAH *on her Kiswahili phrases.*

HOPE. *Pasaka.* [Easter.]

SARAH. *Pasaka.*

The NUNS *sing a Catholic setting of the Kyrie, quietly.*

HOPE. *Pas-a-ka.*

SARAH. *Pas-a-ka.*

HOPE. 'When Christ rose from the tomb', go.

SARAH. *Yesu alipofufuka kutoka kaburini.*

HOPE. Ye*su.*

SARAH. *Yesu.*

HOPE. *Sikiliza*, Sarah, listen, '*Yesu alipofufuka kutoka kaburini.*'

SARAH. *Yesu alipofufuka kutoka kaburini.*

HOPE. *Hamujambo watoto, leo tunajifunza kuhusu pasaka.* 'Hello children, today we're going to learn about Easter'. Go.

SARAH. *Hamujambo watoto, leo tunajifunza kuhusu pasaka...*

HOPE. *Pas-a-ka.*

SARAH. *Pasaka.*

HOPE. When Christ rose from the tomb. Go.

SARAH *is squirming, trying to get it right under* HOPE*'s strict teaching manner, but there is humour. Their friendship is strong.*

SARAH. *Yesu alipofufuka kutoka tumbo.*

HOPE. *Tumbo?*

SARAH. Oh...

HOPE. Stomach?

SARAH *laughs.*

'Tomb', not, 'womb', nincompoop! Go, again.

SARAH *continues working at her desk as* HOPE *leaves.*

SARAH. *Hamujambo watoto, leo tunajifunza kuhusu Pasaka.*

HOPE (*from off*). *Pasaka.*

SARAH. *Pasaka, yesu alipofufuka kutoka kaburini. Kuna yeyote anayeweza kuniambia anachofahamu kuhusu Pasaka?* (*Etc.*)

It's dark, the convent is asleep. The low growl of a leopard cuts the silence. SARAH stiffens. JACK HOLMAN (British, twenty-eight) speaks quietly.

JACK HOLMAN. Stay absolutely still, apologies in advance.

The sound of his rifle firing, blasts through the quiet. The back wall is splattered with blood.

HOPE (*shouting, off*). Sarah?

JACK moves in, checks the beast.

JACK HOLMAN. Got you. (*Alerting those outside.*) He's dead.

The NUNS rush in.

NUNS. Are you all right? – What happened? – Oh my good Lord. – A leopard in your room! (*Etc.*)

JACK takes off his jacket and puts it round SARAH's shoulders.

JACK HOLMAN (*to MOTHER SUPERIOR*). Mother, would you have such a thing as an empty sack?

MOTHER SUPERIOR. Yes.

RUTH. I'll fetch one, Mother.

MOTHER SUPERIOR. Sweet potatoes…

She runs off.

BABETTE. There's so much blood.

MOTHER SUPERIOR. It's still pouring out.

SARAH gets up to help.

JACK HOLMAN (*to SARAH*). Please stay still, surprise does odd things to muscle.

RUTH runs in with a sack and a blanket.

RUTH. Are these big enough?

JACK HOLMAN. Ample. It's just to get a hold of, and they'll soak up some blood. Is anyone feeling strong?

HOPE. Always!

> SARAH *watches the* NUNS *line up with* JACK, *on one side of the leopard.*

JACK HOLMAN. When I say, 'heave'… ready?

NUNS. Ready.

JACK HOLMAN. One, two, three, heave!

> *They push the beast so it rolls onto the sack.*

Well done.

BABETTE. You can feel his muscles.

RUTH. Look at my hands.

HOPE. All his malice, gone!

MOTHER SUPERIOR. We're extremely grateful, Mr Holman.

BABETTE. Shall we help you take him out, Mr Holman?

JACK HOLMAN. Well, if you – I'd appreciate that.

MOTHER SUPERIOR (*to* RUTH, BABETTE *and* HOPE). Sisters, help Mr Holman, then, Hope, put water on the stove and help Sarah clean up.

HOPE. Of course, Mother.

> RUTH, *still stunned, isn't helping.*

MOTHER SUPERIOR. Ruth.

RUTH. Sorry.

JACK HOLMAN. All right, sisters?

NUNS. Yes. (*Etc.*)

JACK HOLMAN. And, heave!

RUTH. Gosh, it's so heavy!

BABETTE. No quibbles about killing the Lord's creature now.

> *They drag the leopard out.*

MOTHER SUPERIOR (*to* SARAH). How are you?

SARAH. Still here.

MOTHER SUPERIOR. That man's a good shot.

SARAH. Isn't he?

MOTHER SUPERIOR. The challenge of a Missionary Sister is an ever unfolding mystery.

SARAH. It's why we do it, isn't it?

MOTHER SUPERIOR. I think so. I think it is.

(*Looking at the chaos of blood.*) How explicit. Grizzly. Clearly, Sarah, you have more to do in this life. I have to admit, I'm glad.

SARAH. Thank you, Mother.

MOTHER SUPERIOR *leaves.* HOPE *comes back with a bucket of water.*

I'll clean up.

HOPE. No you won't.

SARAH. I want to.

HOPE. Not on your own, you won't.

SARAH. I couldn't sleep now anyway.

HOPE. I'll stay awake with you.

SARAH. No.

HOPE. It's too much for one person!

SARAH. Who says?

HOPE. No, Sarah, I won't let you.

SARAH. *Hii chumba yangu, nataka kuisafisha.* [It's my room, I want to clean it.]

HOPE. *Ebu* [come on], I'm your sister.

SARAH. Goodnight.

HOPE. You're being unreasonable, Sarah.

SARAH. *Ebu*, I don't care, go to bed!

> SARAH *pushes* HOPE *out. She looks around her.*

Albert?

> *She takes up* HOPE*'s bucket and stands on the chairs to clean the blood off the wall.* MICHELLE *and* SU-LIN *come on with trays.* SU-LIN *is in full Chinese-maid persona. She points to the mess in* DAVID*'s chisel scar, growling in her made-up Chinese.*

SU-LIN. *Ya tza chin gno tzoo!*

MICHELLE. Translate?

SU-LIN (*in thick accent*). Look at all the mess in this crack, it's unhygienic!

MICHELLE. It's all right, wood kills bacteria. We could do with one of those midget hoovers, couldn't we? Right, you, chairs.

> SU-LIN *approaches each chair as if it was a dangerous animal.* MICHELLE *lays the table.*

Oh, I've set a place for Mr Nobody. Dada-Ben's working, sadly.

> *She removes a knife and fork.* SU-LIN *continues her game as she gathers the chairs.*

Remind me, when I put Ben's spare ribs aside, to save some for next door, they've never tried them. And don't be surprised if 'Grandpa' Gideon doesn't have any, he didn't used to eat meat.

> MICHELLE *fetches the last chair, joining in the game, threatening to make the chair attack* SU-LIN.

ANTHONY (*off*). Here we are. Come in, come in. (*Etc.*)

> MICHELLE *stops short.* ANTHONY *comes in with* GIDEON. *Beat. They look at one another.*

GIDEON. Hello, Michelle.

MICHELLE. Hello, Gideon.

> SU-LIN *rises to greet* GIDEON *in full Chinese persona, singing, with dance movements, her Cantopop song.*

SU-LIN (*singing*).
> *Yu go-ngo gum sung tzu din hai ya go yen*
> *Mo soh why men ya ngo hay tzoy wa sing*
> *U go mo yam zan tzoy foo gno sang woh see*
> *Ho bi tzoi mun soy hey gno.*

> (*Speaking, Chinese accent.*) Hello, pleased to meet you, welcome to our home… (*Etc.*)

GIDEON. Su-Lin, I presume? Pleased to meet you, too.

SU-LIN (*normal accent*). Do you like spare ribs? If you say yes you'll prove Gran wrong, and she's never wrong.

MICHELLE. Su-Lin!

> GIDEON *goes to kiss* MICHELLE's *cheek, offers her daffodils.* SU-LIN *watches them.*

> You found each other, then?

GIDEON. He's the same handsome young thing he always was.

ANTHONY. Well…

SU-LIN. How old was my dad when you last saw him?

GIDEON. A young man.

ANTHONY. Youngish.

MICHELLE (*to* SU-LIN). Before you were born.

ANTHONY. We last saw each other in France.

GIDEON. France, that's right.

SU-LIN. Would you like a chocolate egg to start? If you do, they might let us all have one.

ANTHONY. Just ignore her.

SU-LIN. He can't, he's only just met me.

GIDEON. As far as chocolate starters go, I don't want to offend anyone quite so soon.

MICHELLE. Save the offensive stuff up for later.

It's a joke, but it doesn't work. The atmosphere is awkward.

ANTHONY. Please, take a seat.

SU-LIN. So, do you like spare ribs, or not?

GIDEON *sits.* MICHELLE *and* ANTHONY *start bringing bowls of food in.*

MICHELLE. There's couscous and plenty other things.

GIDEON. Spare couscous?

SU-LIN (*crinkling her nose at his joke*). What? Do you like chicken?

GIDEON. No.

SU-LIN. Halloumi?

GIDEON. Yes.

SU-LIN. Garlic-and-chilli-fried courgettes?

GIDEON. Lovely.

ANTHONY. He doesn't need a tourist guide, Su-Lin, don't crowd your grandpa.

GIDEON. Can I help?

ANTHONY. Thanks.

He passes some dishes. The table is becoming laden with colourful salads and bowls of food.

MICHELLE. There's food for everyone's taste, hopefully.

SU-LIN. Some people don't like lots of different foods on one plate, like different races mixed together.

They all laugh, in their way.

(*To* GIDEON.) Are you African?

GIDEON. I was born in Africa, but I moved away when I was small.

SU-LIN. But you're African to start with?

GIDEON. Not officially. My mother, Sarah, your dad's grandmother – walked out of her home in England, in Staffordshire, you know where Staffordshire is?

SU-LIN. No.

GIDEON. I'll show you after lunch. You got Google maps?

SU-LIN. I've got a world map on my wall.

GIDEON. We could try and find Lichfield on that.

SU-LIN. So, she left home…

GIDEON. And went to live in Africa, where I was born.

SU-LIN. And you're Dad-Ant's dad.

GIDEON. Dad-Ant's, yup.

SU-LIN. It's funny, you being Dad's dad.

MICHELLE. It's new, that's all.

GIDEON. Kind of old and new.

> ANTHONY *and* GIDEON *reach for the food.*

SU-LIN. Wait – *chang cha* – three breaths!

ANTHONY. Actually, it doesn't have to be three…

SU-LIN. I always do three.

ANTHONY (*embarrassed*). Um, we usually just take a moment before eating.

SU-LIN. To say thank you for the food, in our heads.

ANTHONY. To calm down, basically.

GIDEON. Do you?

SU-LIN. Sometimes we forget, or if it's just me and Dad-Ant with cheese and mayonnaise on toast we sometimes skip it, but we always do it on big meals when everyone's here.

GIDEON. I see. Three breaths.

SU-LIN closes her eyes, the others follow. Noises of Africa break in again. JACK HOLMAN is there, at the other end of SARAH's room.

JACK HOLMAN. Excuse me, sister.

She looks up from cleaning her wall.

Jack Holman, I shot the leopard...

SARAH. I know.

JACK HOLMAN. Apologies for the mess. This was the end of a lengthy series of failures, which, when hunting a maneater, can quickly become an inferiority complex, so it's a relief for all of us. I'm only sorry it was your room which ended up being the execution chamber.

SARAH. I'm not.

JACK HOLMAN. He had made nine human kills. Five men, three women, and a boy. And a teenage survivor who doesn't officially count, but you wouldn't want the injuries he's been left with. This was the twelfth consecutive night I've sat up, and I'd been tracking him for fourteen weeks prior to that.

SARAH. Did you follow him here?

JACK HOLMAN. He killed a deer in Moshi last night, so I was sitting over that quarry, anticipating his return. But the truth is he'd become wise to my hunt over the weeks, and reckoned on my being there, so he abandoned his meal. I heard the dogs in Kingori, very uneasy, all of them at the same moment, so. I managed to pick up his pug marks at the edge of the village, and was just in time to see him jump through the high window at the side of your convent.

SARAH. The narrow one?

JACK HOLMAN. Yes.

SARAH. How?

JACK HOLMAN. He'd have returned the same way, sister, silently, with you in his mouth.

SARAH. I'd have screamed...

JACK HOLMAN. The first incision is the throat, so the victim can't scream. He'd have carried you up to four miles that way, stripped every shred of clothing from you, then eaten his quarry at leisure, so, despite the bloody mess, excuse my language, intended purely in the descriptive sense... it is, for certain, the preferable outcome. I'm interrupting you, I'm sorry.

SARAH. Don't be.

JACK HOLMAN. Anyway, I knew I couldn't fail again.

SARAH. You didn't.

JACK HOLMAN. No.

SARAH. I'm alive.

JACK HOLMAN. Indeed. So, thank you for hosting this particular party, sister. I'd better go, transport my prize.

SARAH doesn't respond. It leaves JACK uncertain as to what to do.

I just wanted to check you were well and – retrieve my jacket, if I may?

He takes it, steps back again.

Thank you. Would you like help cleaning? I'd be more than happy to...

From her chair, SARAH unbuttons her dress.

Uh... I'll leave.

She lifts her dress off, over her head. She's in her slip.

Sister, is everything all right with you?

She lifts her slip over her head. He watches. She takes off her briefs, she's naked.

Sister, Sarah, is it?

SARAH. Sarah Best.

JACK HOLMAN. I have to tell you, Sarah Best, that I've been on my own, mostly in the bush, for some months, I'm sleep-deprived, and I feel I might have lost the ability to judge a social situation as perhaps I once did. I just need to tell you that if you don't do anything or say anything in the next ten seconds... then I'm going to put you on that table and take you.

He stands rooted, focused on SARAH.

(*Quietly.*) One, two, three, four, five, six, seven –

SARAH. Ten.

[*The interval for the National Theatre production came here.*]

SECOND HALF

GIDEON *is under the table, curled up.*

SARAH (*singing*).
> Kyrie
> Eleison
> Christe
> Eleison…

SARAH *wipes the table, her waters break.*

Bugger.

She breathes heavily.

(*Calling.*) Hope?

HOPE *arrives. The* NUNS *pick up* SARAH*'s song.* SARAH *is in labour, full swells of contractions sweeping through her as the* NUNS *ricochet off each other vocally.* HOPE *sits with* SARAH, *steady as a rock.*

NUNS (*singing*).
> Kyrie Eleison, Christe Eleison
> Kyrie Eleison, Christe Eleison
> Kyrie Eleison, Christe Eleison… (*Etc.*)

SARAH *labours, leaning on the table, squatting, hanging off it and, finally, she drags the table backwards, shouting.*

SARAH. Uuurghhh!

GIDEON *is revealed.* SARAH *looks at him in awe. He rolls over. He is age six.* SARAH *leaves, taking her nun's habit off.*

GIDEON. Hello, Gideon, hello, table. *Habari*, Gideon? *Habari, meza?*

HOPE *picks up their lesson.*

HOPE. We are very hungry today. Go.

GIDEON. *Leo tuna njaa kama nini.*

HOPE (*correcting his pronunciation*). *'Kama nini.'* Perhaps
Babette has cooked us something delicious, go.

GIDEON. *Labda Shangazi Babette ametutengenezea chakula
kitamu.* Auntie Hope, who's my dad?

HOPE. Why do you ask?

GIDEON. They were talking about him in the village.

HOPE. What did you tell them?

GIDEON. That I don't have one.

HOPE. And what did they say?

GIDEON. That I must have.

HOPE. And what do you think?

GIDEON. I don't know.

HOPE. I don't see one anywhere, do you?

GIDEON. No.

HOPE. You're such a beautiful boy, Gideon.

GIDEON *starts a song* (*traditional Swahili*), *with hand
gestures,* HOPE *joins immediately.*

HOPE *and* GIDEON (*singing*).
    Napolo-Polo
    Napidemu-Deh
    Pollo-Pollo, po!

The CONVENT INHABITANTS *lay the table,* GIDEON
helps.

SARAH. Bless us, O Lord, and these Thy gifts, which we are
about to receive from Thy bounty, through Christ our Lord.

SARAH, GIDEON, *and* NUNS. Amen.

HOPE *serves soup.*

RUTH. What did you do today, Gideon?

GIDEON. Visited Piggy the warthog, and played football in the village.

BABETTE. Did you wear your shoes?

GIDEON (*he didn't*). Mnm...

BABETTE. How many times? You are lucky enough to have shoes, put them on your feet.

GIDEON. Yes, Auntie.

HOPE. We did our four 'R's' with the others, didn't we, Gideon?

GIDEON (*bored*). We always do.

SARAH (*chastising*). Gideon.

RUTH. What did you learn?

HOPE. We read *Janet and John*, we wrote it out in English and Swahili, we worked out sums with sticks and stones, and then Gideon wanted to build a big house with sticks, so he did, then, 'religion', well –

MOTHER SUPERIOR. Will you shut up, Sister Hope.

Beat.

HOPE. Mother, is something troubling you?

MOTHER SUPERIOR. Sister Ruth, can you pass the water, please? If there is something troubling me, sister, I will take the issue up with God.

HOPE. Of course, Reverend Mother. I wasn't being curious, Mother, I just wondered if there was something I could help with?

MOTHER SUPERIOR. There's nothing you can do, sister.

HOPE. Forgive me, Mother, I didn't –

MOTHER SUPERIOR. Enough.

HOPE. I didn't mean to –

MOTHER SUPERIOR. I mean enough.

HOPE. I know, I only –

MOTHER SUPERIOR. Silence for twenty-four hours, sister!

HOPE. But, Mother…

MOTHER SUPERIOR. From *now*.

Silence.

GIDEON. What did you do today, Mother Aoife?

MOTHER SUPERIOR. Well, Gideon, the best part of my day was seeing the sun rise. Because, this afternoon, I learned that there are to be some changes round here and that we have to alter our current arrangement.

GIDEON. Can we have pets in the house?

SARAH *drops her spoon.*

MOTHER SUPERIOR. I had a visit from a brother in Dar es Salaam. It seems the Diocesan Bishop has heard about our living situation and, not surprisingly, he's not best pleased. The long and short of it is that it is no longer feasible –

BABETTE. Excuse me, Mother, but should we be having this conversation here?

HOPE *is in misery, unable to speak.*

MOTHER SUPERIOR. Sister Babette, do you suppose I would be speaking about these things if I thought we shouldn't be? Together, at this table.

BABETTE. No, Mother, forgive me.

GIDEON. What's everyone saying?

RUTH. Sarah is the most zealous of us all, Mother…

MOTHER SUPERIOR. Unfortunately, however, she's not a noviciate any more.

RUTH. She's the best teacher.

MOTHER SUPERIOR. We are a religious community.

SARAH. You are my family.

MOTHER SUPERIOR. We can no longer house you, and, in truth, we never should have.

RUTH. Do they know about his father, how she met him here?

GIDEON. When?

BABETTE. Not now, Gideon.

MOTHER SUPERIOR. Believe me when I tell you, Sarah, it grieves me more than I can say.

GIDEON. I don't like it.

MOTHER SUPERIOR. We'll assist you all we can, to find somewhere in the village.

RUTH. With due respect, Mother, if they understood how integral Sarah was –

MOTHER SUPERIOR. The respect that is due to a Mother Superior from her nuns is obedience and unquestioning support, Sister Ruth.

HOPE. But we help unmarried mothers!

MOTHER SUPERIOR. *Silence.* It is not appropriate to house an illegitimate child, I should not have capitulated.

GIDEON. We like God, too.

MOTHER SUPERIOR. We made an exception, we can do so no longer.

SARAH. When?

MOTHER SUPERIOR. By the end of the week.

GIDEON *drops off his chair.*

SARAH (*hard*). How much is the voyage to England?

BABETTE. England?

RUTH. You can't do that, Sarah!

BABETTE. There's no one there for you.

MOTHER SUPERIOR. You've no house.

BABETTE (*to* MOTHER SUPERIOR). She couldn't get the money back, could she?

SARAH. Of course not.

RUTH. Surely the church –

SARAH. It was a gift.

MOTHER SUPERIOR. Sarah, we can absorb some of your living costs, but you have to stay close.

RUTH. You can't take Gideon...

SARAH. Can't I?

> GIDEON *approaches* MOTHER SUPERIOR *as a tortoise.*

MOTHER SUPERIOR. What are you doing there, Gideon?

> *He licks her with his tortoise tongue.*

Licking! How dare you lick, you know licking is out of bounds!

> GIDEON *retreats.*

Come out from under that table.

GIDEON. I can't, I'm a tortoise, you can't take tortoises to England.

SARAH. Be quiet, Gideon, you'll go where you're told.

MOTHER SUPERIOR. Sarah.

SARAH. Yes, Aoife?

> GIDEON *bucks the table.*

Stop shoving or I'll leave without you!

> *The* NUNS *go, leaving* SARAH, HOPE *and* GIDEON. *Days later.*

HOPE. Come out now, Gideon, please stop playing.

SARAH. We'll miss the bloody boat, Gideon!

He kicks out, chairs fall.

Ow! How dare you? I will kick you back, you little beast.

GIDEON. I'm not coming!

SARAH. You are, face it!

HOPE. Sarah!

HOPE *gets under the table with him.*

Your mother has tickets, you have to go.

GIDEON. How come you stay?

HOPE. I wish you were staying too.

GIDEON. Not at the convent, though.

HOPE. You need to go to England, see your family.

GIDEON. They're dead.

HOPE. Find your grandmother, maybe?

GIDEON. Why?

SARAH (*imperative*). Gideon, get out from under there now!

He sings to block her out.

GIDEON (*singing*).
   / *Napolo-Polo*
   Napidemu-Deh
   Pollo-Pollo.

SARAH. Gideon, listen to me. They think you are a dirty little
   boy and that you're the son of a whore. That is why we're
   going.

He stops singing.

GIDEON. A what?

HOPE. Sarah, you're so severe! It's not true, Gideon.

GIDEON. Is it true, Hope?

HOPE. No. *Nakuomba tafadhali* [please], Sarah.

SARAH. *Nakuomba tafadhali* what?

HOPE. Stay! We can find somewhere, I will help. You don't have to go.

SARAH. We don't need your help.

HOPE. That's your arrogance speaking, Sarah.

SARAH. *Ebu.* [So / Oh come now.]

HOPE. You are proud as a bull, it's unnecessary. Mother Superior wants you to stay, her hands are tied. God wants you to stay, Gideon wants to stay, don't you, Gideon?

GIDEON. Do you want us?

HOPE. Of course I want you!

GIDEON. I'm staying with Hope.

SARAH. Then I'm going without you.

HOPE. Sarah. We have to rise above our wounds!

SARAH (*at the end of her tether*). Yes, and nurse ourselves!

SARAH *starts walking.* GIDEON *panics.*

GIDEON. Mummy…

HOPE. Gideon, you have to leave, we can't have you here.

GIDEON. Why?

HOPE. Because we live in a house of God and…

She addresses him with the fire of her anger.

I have never felt so miserable in any moment before this. It can't be right, or what God would want. The sun doesn't rise, Gideon, without me thinking of you. I cannot begin to imagine life when you're no longer here, your serious, beautiful face. But your mother loves you and she is going to England and you must go with her.

GIDEON. Why don't you come too?

HOPE. Look at me. I will always, always be with you. Whenever you feel sad, please remember, 'Hope is with me.' Don't forget, 'Hope is with me.' Go.

GIDEON. *Hope yuko na mimi.*

HOPE. My Gideon, I will miss you so much.

The London family flood in and refill the table.

Part Three

HOPE *leaves*. SU-LIN *sings to* GIDEON.

SU-LIN (*singing*).
    Yu go-ngo gum sung tzu din hai ya go yen
    Mo soh why men ya ngo hay tzoy wa sing
    U go mo yam zan tzoy foo gno sang woh see
    Ho bi tzoi mun soy hey gno.

GIDEON. Got it.

SU-LIN. Could you pass the ribs, please.

The grown-ups have finished eating.

GIDEON. Sure.

SU-LIN. Can you help me break one off?

GIDEON. Course.

He gets his hands messy.

SU-LIN. *Cheking ow, ching gnow* (*Etc.*) ['Thank you' *in her made-up language.*]

GIDEON. So, what about your other grandpa, Su-Lin, Ben's dad, does he come round much?

SU-LIN. He's round all the time.

MICHELLE. He's very jolly company.

SU-LIN. When are you going home?

ANTHONY. It's not polite to ask people how long they're staying, Su-Lin.

SU-LIN. I don't mean when's he leaving here, I meant when's he going home!

GIDEON. It's fine. Uh, well, I don't really have a home, I've been on the move for many years.

SU-LIN. Like, where?

GIDEON. Ooh, like Kyrgyzstan, Sumatra, India, Thailand, Brazil.

SU-LIN (*giggling*). I'm not from Thailand! I thought you looked at me like I was from Thailand, but I'm not.

ANTHONY. Your granddad knows your mix, Su-Lin.

MICHELLE. Is that my water?

GIDEON. I don't know. It's not mine.

ANTHONY. I always have everything – red, white, water, I'm decision-phobic.

GIDEON. Is that a dig?

ANTHONY. No.

SU-LIN *is fidgeting*.

MICHELLE. Su-Lin, what's got in to you today?

SU-LIN. I'm hot.

MICHELLE. Take your cardigan off then, monkey.

GIDEON. You know, Su-Lin, I used to have a pet tortoise when I was young, called Charlie?

SU-LIN. Did you?

GIDEON. And one time I was out in the yard with him I heard this, 'tink', sound. I couldn't work out what it was. Each time I looked away, it would happen again, 'tink'.

MICHELLE *starts clearing the table.*

(*To* MICHELLE.) Thank you, that was delicious, by the way. (*To* SU-LIN.) Do you know what it turned out to be?

SU-LIN. What?

GIDEON. A monkey, throwing nuts at his shell.

SU-LIN. Really?

GIDEON. Honest, target practice. I finally caught him doing it, and he was this big. (*Shows her how small.*) A little, long-tailed monkey, and I swear to you he was laughing, like this. 'Tink!', 'ho, ho, ho, ho, ho!' (*Etc.*)

SU-LIN. Tink, ho, ho, ho, ho, ho, ho, ho. Did you throw them back?

MICHELLE. Don't talk with your mouth full, Su-Lin.

SU-LIN. What?

ANTHONY. Don't talk with your mouth full at table. (*To* GIDEON.) Have you been back to Africa much?

GIDEON. Recently, for the first time.

MICHELLE. Did you go to Tanzania?

GIDEON. The convent's gone, but… I did. (*To* SU-LIN.) Went to find my father, Jack.

ANTHONY. Really?

MICHELLE. What prompted that?

GIDEON. Getting older?

SU-LIN. Is that the hunter?

GIDEON. Yeah. Though he'd not picked up a gun in a while.

SU-LIN. Why not, too old?

GIDEON. No…

SU-LIN. Why then? If I was a hunter I'd never stop.

GIDEON. After a visit to England once, he started drinking alcohol for the first time. He was driving home one night when he knocked something over in the dark. Turned out it was one of the locals. He was so mortified, he handed himself in to the police, never drove, never drank, and never picked up a gun again.

MICHELLE. Not at all single-minded like your mum, then.

GIDEON. I only just learnt all this.

MICHELLE. How was it to see him?

GIDEON. Important.

SU-LIN. Can I get down? I'm not very hungry.

MICHELLE. You will be later.

GIDEON. When the chocolate comes out.

SU-LIN. Look, a daddy-long-legs!

MICHELLE. All you've eaten is ribs, Su-Lin.

SU-LIN. I'm too hot to eat.

ANTHONY. Go on then, take that daddy-long-legs into the garden, I'll be out shortly, okay?

SU-LIN. Nice to meet you.

GIDEON. It's running away...

She catches the daddy-long-legs.

And you, Su-Lin, a real pleasure.

SU-LIN. *Ching ching cha chow! (Etc.)*

She goes.

GIDEON. Quite a girl.

ANTHONY. Her mother's very spirited.

MICHELLE (*to* ANTHONY). They're your genes too.

ANTHONY. Poor kid.

GIDEON. Is she not around at all, her mother?

ANTHONY. No, it was always purely a surrogacy relationship. We were very fortunate with Min, her birth mum.

MICHELLE. Fortunate and patient.

ANTHONY. It was a long haul, but Ben is very steady, calls all my dithering, hubris. He runs this homeless charity, you know, he's very practical, just gets on with stuff, and Mum completely helped keep me sane.

MICHELLE. You asked, though, love.

ANTHONY. Big deal, 'Help!'

MICHELLE. If you're too proud to ask....

GIDEON. She's a gorgeous kid.

MICHELLE. I know.

ANTHONY. She brings so much to our lives.

GIDEON. Kids do.

(*To* MICHELLE.) So, do you live nearby?

MICHELLE. Mm, I'm here most days.

GIDEON. That's nice.

MICHELLE. Well, both boys work.

ANTHONY. Wish we didn't.

MICHELLE. And I offer.

GIDEON. I'd love to offer, myself.

ANTHONY (*surprised*). You'll stop in London a while, will you?

GIDEON. I'm not sure what my plans are, yet.

MICHELLE. Back to Brazil?

GIDEON. No, not Brazil.

MICHELLE. Where, then?

GIDEON. I don't know. (*To* ANTHONY.) I've missed you.

MICHELLE. You bet you damn well missed him!

MICHELLE starts clearing the table.

GIDEON. Michelle, I'm sorry if this is threatening for you.

MICHELLE. Finished?

She snatches up his glass.

ANTHONY. Let me do that, Mum. Dad's just trying to reconnect…

MICHELLE. Your dad wants coffee, Anthony, go and make your father some coffee.

ANTHONY. Coffee?

GIDEON. Why not.

ANTHONY. Right. And tea for you?

MICHELLE. No, coffee, black, three sugars.

ANTHONY goes. MICHELLE confronts GIDEON.

How long are you staying, Gideon?

The table is covered with a batik cloth. Herefordshire, 1964. AISHA (fifteen), BARBARA (twelve), JULIAN (forties), ORION (forties), STACEY (forties) and CHRIS (thirties) pile round. Their years since leaving the convent have left SARAH guarded and GIDEON tense. SARAH (forty-four) places a cake with lit candles in front of GIDEON (thirteen).

SARAH. Gideon? Happy birthday, Gid.

The others give hugs and their blessing in quick succession.

ORION. *Lá breithe shona dhuit.* ['Happy birthday' *in Gaelic*.]

JULIAN. May the doctor never earn a penny from you.

STACEY. May the road rise up to meet you.

CHRIS. Thirteen, dream-machine.

AISHA. Age doesn't matter, unless you are a cheese.

BARBARA. I don't know what to say.

AISHA. Go on, Gid, blow them out!

He blows, the cake catches fire.

SARAH. Shit, oh shit!

AISHA. Shit!

GIDEON. Mum...

JULIAN. Don't panic...

Everyone crowds round, trying to blow it out.

STACEY. Here, my tea, whoops!

She pours her tea on it, the flames subside.

GIDEON. My cake.

STACEY. You've heard of tea cake, haven't you?

AISHA. Was it my decorations?

ORION. What were they?

AISHA. Really cute flowers made of tissue paper.

JULIAN. Cute but combustible.

AISHA. Sorry, Gideon.

GIDEON. S'okay, I don't really mind.

JULIAN. See these youngsters? Courteous-living in action.

ORION. In the face of cake-vandalism.

AISHA. I didn't do it on purpose!

She hits ORION. *It's all in good humour.*

JULIAN. That's what all vandals say.

STACEY. You need to make the first cut, Gideon, the quicker
we eat it, the less the tea will seep in.

GIDEON. Who do I wish to?

JULIAN. Good question.

ORION. The fabulous cake elves.

AISHA. Do you believe in guardian angels?

SARAH. No.

JULIAN. Just send it out there, never mind who to.

ORION. To the communal pool of good.

> GIDEON *wishes and cuts.*

GIDEON. Urgh, it's soggy…

STACEY. Better than crispy.

SARAH. Is that knife big enough?

AISHA. What d'you wish for, Gid?

GIDEON. Do I have to say?

STACEY. No.

JULIAN. I like this cloth, is it Indian?

> SARAH *doesn't answer, hands out the cake.*

ORION. You wouldn't see that in Ross market.

JULIAN, ORION, AISHA, STACEY, GIDEON, BARBARA,
CHRIS (*re: cake*). Thanks. – Thank you. (*Etc*.)

When they all have some, they sing.

ALL (*singing*).
> With humble hearts we eat, with friendly hearts we share,
> with thankful words we say, thank the cook!

With a cheer, ORION *takes a bow. They eat cake.*

STACEY. Thirteen. That's an important rite of passage.

ORION. Maybe we should shave your head, Gideon.

JULIAN. Do you feel like a man?

GIDEON. Not really.

JULIAN. You know if there's anything you ever want to talk about, about growing up or anything, I'm here, we're all here, should you need us.

GIDEON. Thanks.

SARAH. Thank you.

BARBARA. Where were you last birthday?

GIDEON. In Leeds, in this council shelter, but Mum wasn't home yet by the time I woke up and they made me go to school before she got back, so.

SARAH. We had a cake after school, though, didn't we.

GIDEON. We left there soon after.

JULIAN. Who's on milking rota this week?

STACEY. I am, why?

Indicating the milk in his tea.

JULIAN. It's very goaty, this, have you noticed?

AISHA. Cos it's his birthday, can Gideon sleep in my dorm tonight?

Everyone looks at her.

I'd like to teach him more about the commune. Cos I think his mum's really quiet, you're quite quiet, Sarah, and maybe he'd like someone to talk to.

ORION. I don't think you're particularly quiet.

AISHA. I didn't mean any offence.

SARAH. None taken, Aisha.

JULIAN. What about Babs?

AISHA. She can stay, or go next door, I don't mind.

   BARBARA *shrugs.*

SARAH. What do you think, Gid?

GIDEON. I'd like that.

SARAH. Yeah?

GIDEON. Yeah.

Beat.

SARAH. I know I don't say much.

JULIAN. You don't have to.

SARAH. But I'll say now that I'm very grateful to be here. I respect your way of living, I like hard work, so thank you for offering us this chance.

JULIAN. You're very welcome.

ORION. Ditto.

SARAH. I hope we'll prove valuable.

ORION. No question about it, after tasting your curry.

GIDEON. Basically, this was our last option.

JULIAN. Well.

GIDEON. No, it was.

ORION. That's fine.

GIDEON. We had nowhere left to try. That wasn't run by Catholics, anyway. But it's good here.

AISHA. Cool.

JULIAN (*re: table*). It's a decent size, this, isn't it? You could meet around that.

AISHA. But we sit on the floor in meetings!

JULIAN. I know, I'm just saying.

SARAH. You can use it, I don't mind.

JULIAN. I didn't mean –

SARAH. Honestly.

ORION. Maybe we could try, see if it works?

JULIAN. Sure.

JULIAN puts a hand familiarly on SARAH's arm.

Thanks, Sarah.

SARAH. Pleasure.

CHRIS. I need to get to town, do my 'real world' shift.

ORION. Are you taking the car?

CHRIS. Yeah, I'll pick up the dry goods after work. Happy birthday, Gid.

Everyone starts to go.

ALL. Happy birthday, Gid. – Happy birthday! – See you later.

STACEY. Happy birthday, Gideon.

A few months later. A meeting is in process round the table with the same people.

GIDEON. Do you want to speak, Stacey?

He offers her a large stone, she doesn't take it.

JULIAN. Gideon, may I have the speak-stone?

GIDEON passes it to him.

It's unfair to prompt others, Gideon, people speak when they have something to say, and the stone protects their communication, okay? I'd like to bring the barn in to focus today, discuss ideas for development, potential uses, possible income from it, I know this is contentious, and also look at the maintenance fund and the realities of those strictures on it.

GIDEON reaches to take the stone.

GIDEON. But what if I know they do have something to say?

The stone passes back and forth between the speakers.

JULIAN. Then they'll voice it in their own good time.

AISHA *reaches for the stone.*

AISHA. Yeah, but we have to trust each other and bring things in to the open, so I think Stacey should say whatever it is, because Gideon's acting weirdly and I'd like to know why.

She passes STACEY *the stone.*

GIDEON. Why don't you say it?

ORION. Stone…

GIDEON (*taking it*). Is there something you'd like to say, Stacey?

STACEY. Not really, honey, no.

GIDEON. Then maybe I should.

SARAH *reaches for the stone.*

SARAH. Before you do, Gid, can I just ask – (*To* STACEY.) Stella, are we cool?

A snigger goes round.

JULIAN. We're allowed to laugh, guys, it's okay.

SARAH (*appalled*). I mean…

STACEY. My name's Stacey.

SARAH. I know, of course I know, I don't know where my head is.

JULIAN. It happens.

CHRIS. Just a weird blip.

SARAH. I was just going to ask, um – Stacey, are you angry with me?

STACEY *looks at her.* ORION *takes the stone.*

ORION. I'd like to acknowledge that question, Sarah. Truthfully, this is what these meetings are about, and, in practice, it's hard, we have to overcome real barriers to saying it how we think it is, bravo.

JULIAN. I agree.

STACEY. Do you?

JULIAN. We heard some of your anger last time, Stacey, is there more?

STACEY. I wasn't angry last time, I was miffed.

SARAH. At me?

AISHA. Can I just say, you grown-ups are completely ignoring us! Gideon was about to say something, and now you're just having some completely random, different conversation!

JULIAN. Yup, fair cop, fair cop.

ORION. You want the stone, Gideon?

STACEY *takes it.*

STACEY. What he was about to say, seeing as you're all so interested, is that he and I, Gideon and I, had sex, didn't we, Gideon?

Silence.

AISHA. Is that true, Gideon? Did you have sex with Stacey?

GIDEON (*with the stone*). Well, not just that – we're together now, aren't we?

AISHA. Why is she laughing?

STACEY. I'm not – (*She is.*) I'm sorry. Sorry, Gideon.

AISHA *grabs the stone, holds it.*

AISHA. I think that I don't want to stay here any more. You're older than his mum, and I'm going now.

SARAH *takes the stone.*

SARAH. Sit down, Aisha, this is to do with me, I'm sure.

GIDEON. Not everything's about you, you know! God.

JULIAN. Observe the stone, Gideon.

SARAH (*to* STACEY, *with the stone*). If you wanted to shock me, you have, but I wasn't aware of you having a relationship with Julian, if that's what this is about.

JULIAN *grabs the stone*.

JULIAN. We're not 'in' a relationship, we have relations, sometimes.

GIDEON. What?

STACEY. Quite often, in fact, we have 'related' over the years, you and I, Julian, haven't we? Forget to mention it to Sarah?

JULIAN *speaks with the stone*.

JULIAN. Seeing as the whole principle upon which this living situation is based – autonomy, emancipation from social norm – I didn't feel it was necessary.

GIDEON. What the fuck is going on?

AISHA. This is getting way heavy…

ORION. Don't worry.

JULIAN. There's never been a thing here, you *know* that, Stacey, the thing we've tried to get away from in the outside world, where 'this woman is mine, that man is mine'.

SARAH. Belonging.

GIDEON. So instead you just have anyone you want?

STACEY. Answer the boy – sorry, Gideon – man!

JULIAN (*to* STACEY). I really do feel bad you're hurting, that wasn't my intention.

SARAH. I thought you'd know the rules better than anyone, Stacey, you've had five years –

STACEY. And you've had five minutes, so fuck off!

GIDEON. That's my mum you're talking to!

JULIAN. I thought everyone understood the rules of play.

ORION *takes the stone*.

ORION. The only person you belong to is yourself.

GIDEON *grabs the stone*.

GIDEON. She's totally fucking lying anyway, we didn't do anything, she told me to say it in the meeting just to confuse everybody.

STACEY. Don't feel bad, Gideon, it was beautiful, it was fabulous, you're a lamb.

GIDEON. Like I'd do that, Aisha.

SARAH. I don't understand what I've done to you, Stacey.

STACEY. Then you're really thick.

GIDEON *takes off his top*.

GIDEON. I'm hot!

SARAH (*to* STACEY). Gideon is thirteen... (*To* GIDEON.) You're thirteen, you can do what you like but, in my opinion, that's not the best thing to be doing.

GIDEON. Like I care, like I care.

ORION. Stone.

STACEY. Gideon, we fucked, it's okay, worse things happen.

GIDEON. As if I'd do that!

STACEY. In denial already, I wonder where that comes from?

ORION *takes the stone*.

ORION. It's actually against the law, Stacey, so, I don't really know what you were thinking of.

STACEY. Soft skin?

GIDEON *grabs the stone, offers it to* AISHA.

GIDEON. I want Aisha to speak. (*About* STACEY.) She's a psycho, Aisha, honestly.

JULIAN. You can't force people, Gideon.

AISHA *takes the stone*.

AISHA. I want to speak. Cos, if you'd kept your thing in your trousers, Julian, and not screwed around, she wouldn't have felt angry and gone and, gone and whatever with Gideon. You're sick, all of you are sick.

GIDEON (*to* SARAH). You've just messed everything up!

SARAH. Don't turn on me.

JULIAN (*going towards* GIDEON). That's not fair on your mother, Gideon.

GIDEON. Fuck off, fuck off, keep away from me.

ORION. The kid's angry.

JULIAN. Speak with the stone, guys…

AISHA *takes the stone*.

AISHA. I think you're a fucking bitch, Stacey, and you should leave.

STACEY. I think –

ORION. Stone.

STACEY *takes it,* AISHA *grabs it back*.

AISHA. I think you spoil things for other people and Julian calls you a cunt behind your back.

JULIAN *seizes the stone*.

JULIAN. Those are untrue, spiteful words, Aisha, you know I love Stacey. The last thing I ever meant was to cause hurt.

STACEY. Isn't it funny how things turn out?

ORION *takes the stone*.

ORION. However it feels right now, this has been a really productive meeting. I know we didn't discuss the barn, but we've definitely managed to clear the air of some tensions, flush them out.

AISHA. I think you're a cunt as well, Gideon.

GIDEON. Mum, tell her I didn't do anything wrong!

SARAH. I can't mother you any more.

JULIAN. Please, guys, the stone.

SARAH. You should know what's what at your age.

JULIAN. We only speak when we're holding the stone.

ORION *has put the stone in the middle of the table.*

GIDEON. Go on then, table, you were there, you've always been there, you speak. See? It doesn't work, the speak-stone doesn't work, none of it bloody works!

Everyone has gone. GIDEON *(nineteen) and* SARAH *(forty-nine) are left.* SARAH *rolls a joint.*

She likes films and knows loads of things, but she says I'm the most interesting person she's ever met, and stuff.

SARAH. She must like you, Gid.

GIDEON. She says I'm like from another planet.

SARAH. You've met someone with different experiences, that's all right, it's only term two.

GIDEON. I don't feel well. I feel like I want to punch someone really hard. I'm a peaceful person but I get filled with this rage.

SARAH. Right. Is that because of Michelle?

GIDEON. It feels wrong to be here, I should be there. I keep thinking about Michelle, I want to make everything okay in her life, I want to be the best for her.

SARAH. You are, you're Gideon Best.

GIDEON. No, the *best*.

SARAH. The best what?

He can't answer.

GIDEON. We make each other laugh, and laugh, like, all night.
And she really likes the things I do to her. I don't think she'd
ever done it before.

SARAH. Are you careful?

GIDEON. What do you mean?

SARAH. Not to get pregnant?

GIDEON. Oh, I think she sorts that. It's like there's a fire
between us, but also like I belong to a different life to her.
You know with Aisha sometimes I feel like she's my sister or
something, but with Michelle… (*Matter of factly.*) There's
never a moment when I don't want to fuck her. She makes
me inside out. It's hot.

He takes off his top.

SARAH. Do you want something to eat?

GIDEON. Yes, please. Where's Aisha?

SARAH. Trimming the big tree with Orion.

GIDEON. We've been studying how you can use tree resin to
mix cement.

SARAH. Have you?

GIDEON. Yeah.

SARAH. Sounds good.

GIDEON. It's brilliant. What's 'Amor Patris' mean?

SARAH. What?

GIDEON. 'Amor Patris, J.H.'

SARAH. Where?

GIDEON. Here.

On one of the table legs. SARAH goes quiet.

Have you ever been to Spain?

SARAH. Sorry?

GIDEON. Spain.

SARAH. No.

GIDEON. Michelle's going.

SARAH. You want to go to Spain?

GIDEON. We haven't got the money, it's fine. Who wrote this, Mum?

No response.

Mum? I don't recognise the writing. Mum?

SARAH. Mmn?

GIDEON. Who wrote it, who's J.H.?

SARAH. Jack Holman.

GIDEON. Who?

SARAH. Must be Jack.

GIDEON. Who's Jack?

SARAH. Your father.

GIDEON. What?

SARAH. Must be his writing.

GIDEON. How?

SARAH. He visited.

GIDEON. When?

SARAH. While you were away.

GIDEON. Just now, this term?

SARAH. Mm.

GIDEON. Did you phone halls? I can get here from Northampton...

SARAH. I know you can.

GIDEON. Where does he live, Mum, is he living here?

SARAH. He lives in Africa.

GIDEON. That's where he did live.

SARAH. He still does.

GIDEON. So, why was he here, in England, Mum? Mum!

SARAH. I'm not deaf, Gideon! He came to see you.

GIDEON. How come he didn't, then?

SARAH. Because I asked him to leave.

GIDEON. Why?

SARAH. There was no point him being here.

GIDEON *looks at her.*

GIDEON. Did you tell him where I was?

SARAH. No.

GIDEON. But I've never met him.

SARAH. You don't need to.

GIDEON. But he's my dad.

SARAH. You don't need a dad.

GIDEON. I'd like a dad! Is he married?

SARAH. No.

GIDEON. Do I have brothers and sisters?

SARAH. No.

GIDEON. Just me?

SARAH. Yes.

GIDEON. Always, ever?

SARAH. Yes.

GIDEON. I'm hot, my throat hurts.

SARAH. So go outside.

GIDEON. I'm hot on the inside.

SARAH. So am I, Gideon, now will you just go.

GIDEON. Why?

SARAH. I'm busy. Go on, go outside, go!

GIDEON. I'm going, shit, shit!

SARAH. Get out of my hair!

GIDEON. I always, always hoped one day I would meet my dad.

SARAH *shouts at him, exasperated.*

SARAH. We take our thing and we live with it, Gideon.

GIDEON. I'm going back to Northampton. I'm going to Northampton, I am, I'm going. Bye, Mum. Bye. Bye. Bye. (*Etc.*)

SARAH *stays.* JACK (*forty-eight*) *appears.*

JACK HOLMAN. All right, I understand, when is my allotted time up?

SARAH. 11.32.

JACK HOLMAN. That's very precise. So I have twenty more minutes?

SARAH. Nineteen.

JACK HOLMAN. And where's the perimeter, where exactly do I have to be in nineteen minutes?

SARAH. Out of here.

JACK HOLMAN. Why did you call him Gideon?

SARAH. I don't know.

JACK HOLMAN. It's an unexpected name for a nun.

SARAH. I'm not a nun.

JACK HOLMAN. But you were.

SARAH. Eighteen.

JACK HOLMAN. It's my middle name, I just wondered if somebody had told you that?

SARAH. No.

Silence.

JACK HOLMAN. Seventeen.

SARAH. You've got the same, um, lip thing...

JACK HOLMAN. Have we?

SARAH. Mmm. I didn't know about the name.

JACK HOLMAN. Have you been happy?

SARAH. You have to go.

JACK HOLMAN. If I write a message, will you give it to him?

SARAH. No.

JACK HOLMAN. Would it be so bad, to discover you have a father? I know it's belated, but I'd really like to –

SARAH. We don't need a family. Sixteen.

JACK HOLMAN. I'm reluctant to leave.

SARAH. Oh, well.

JACK HOLMAN. Do you have some message for Hope? She remembers you very fondly.

It's painful for SARAH *to remember.*

SARAH. Hope.

JACK HOLMAN. She runs an orphanage on the other side of the lake, she'd love to hear from you.

SARAH *shakes her head.*

Nothing?

SARAH. No.

JACK HOLMAN. Do you have a photo?

SARAH. Of?

JACK HOLMAN. Gideon?

SARAH. Yes, thank you. Fifteen.

JACK HOLMAN. If you give me a photograph, I'll go, if you don't, I won't see fit to.

SARAH exits. JACK immediately takes his ink pen out and writes on the table leg. SARAH comes back, hands JACK the photo. He absorbs it.

I see what you mean about the lip thing.

He looks at her.

SARAH. Some things are best left pure.

There's a moment of peace between them.

It's time for you to leave.

JACK HOLMAN. I'm going. Thank you for the photograph, I appreciate it.

His warmth unnerves her. She retaliates.

SARAH. Ten, nine, eight, seven, six, five...

JACK HOLMAN. One.

JACK leaves. GIDEON picks up again.

GIDEON. Bye, Mum, I'm going.

SARAH fetches a tool bag.

Bye.

She takes an axe to the table leg with JACK's writing on.

SARAH. Urgh!

GIDEON. Bye.

It's hard work. She tries a saw. Her noise alerts the commune, JULIAN, CHRIS and AISHA come in.

JULIAN. Hi.

SARAH. Hi.

JULIAN. What are you doing?

SARAH. Chopping the leg off.

JULIAN. Why?

SARAH. I'm chopping off all the legs.

JULIAN. Because…?

SARAH. We can sit on the floor and at table.

She saws and saws.

JULIAN. Do you want help?

SARAH. Yes, please.

AISHA. Mental!

JULIAN *grins. They set about sawing all four legs off.*

JULIAN, CHRIS *and* AISHA. How many saws have we got? – Hold that! – Can you get the other end? – Great. – Mind your fingers. – Come on, Chris! – Nearly through… – It's not a race! – Last one. – Teamwork! – Look at that. – Fabulous! (*Etc.*)

SARAH *laughs as one by one the legs come off.*

SARAH. Cut them off, cut them all off, who needs them, any of them?

JULIAN. You're in a naughty mood, Sarah! I'll have to come and see you later.

SARAH. And saw off my legs?

JULIAN. Find out what's holding them together, first.

The table clunks to the ground as the last of the legs is sawn through.

JULIAN, CHRIS *and* AISHA. Hurray!

Young ALBERT (*eight*) *is there.*

ALBERT (*singing*).
> Oh, Jemima, where's your Uncle Jim?
> He's under the water, teaching the fucks to swim.
> First he does the breaststroke, then he does the side,
> And now he's under the water swimming against the tide.

JULIAN, CHRIS *and* AISHA *move the table away from the debris. They leave.*

Come on, Sarah.

SARAH *climbs on to the low table to join* ALBERT. *She is a child again.* ALBERT *rows the table like a boat.*

SARAH. Where are we going?

ALBERT. Where do you want to go?

SARAH. A big lake surrounded by mountains.

ALBERT. We can do that, we can go anywhere.

> (*Singing.*)
> Oh don't be unkind to a fuck
> Cos a fuck may be somebody's brother
> They always live in the swamp
> Where the weather is always fuck.

As he sings, they play, shoving each other back and forth.

Sshh.

SARAH. What?

ALBERT. Can you hear that?

SARAH. What?

ALBERT (*quacking*). Wah, wah – it's a fuck.

SARAH. Wah, wah.

ALBERT. We're surrounded! Swim away, Sarah, swim! Wah, wah, wah, wah – (*Etc.*)

They swim away like ducks.

SARAH *and* ALBERT. Wah, wah, wah, wah, wah, wah, wah wah – (*Etc.*)

MICHELLE (*twenty-nine*), GIDEON (*thirty*) *and* ANTHONY (*nine*) *gather.*

GIDEON. That's what she said, is it, 'scatter my ashes where I wasted my life'?

MICHELLE. Gideon…

JULIAN. You need to calm down, Gideon –

GIDEON. You need to fuck off, Julian.

MICHELLE. Gideon.

GIDEON. Sorry. Sorry, little man. My mum's dead, I'm feeling sad.

JULIAN. We don't have to shout when we're sad.

GIDEON. You think you're a fucking guru, you always have.

MICHELLE. Gideon!

GIDEON. Sorry, sorry, Ant. (*To* JULIAN.) Look, will you step outside, can we step outside for five minutes?

JULIAN. Sure.

GIDEON. Cos I've got a kid here, you know?

JULIAN. Of course.

ORION *appears.*

ORION. The fire's going.

JULIAN. Good, great.

GIDEON. Which fire?

ORION. Sarah's fire.

ORION *hugs* GIDEON. GIDEON *pushes him off.*

GIDEON. You are not subjecting her to any more hippy shit, do you hear?

ORION. Perfectly, Gideon, couldn't be clearer.

GIDEON. Where are the ashes?

ORION. Beside the fire.

They move off, the argument rages on.

JULIAN (*off*). Like it or not, this is where your mum lived and died.

GIDEON (*off*). Because she was sunk!

ORION (*off*). No, she believed in intentional living, Gideon.

GIDEON (*off*). Crap, she'd just run out of gumption. She'd have left years ago.

JULIAN (*off*). That's very damning, and not fair to your mother.

MICHELLE. You okay, love?

ANTHONY. Yeah. Dad's voice is loud.

MICHELLE. I know. Where do you think Gran's ashes should go?

ANTHONY. I don't know.

MICHELLE. She did love the woods.

ANTHONY. And the mountains. She told me about her favourite mountain, once.

MICHELLE. In Tanzania?

ANTHONY. Yeah, and that massive lake.

JULIAN (*off*). She couldn't have been more clear, Gideon, she wanted her remains let loose in the forest.

GIDEON (*off*). Well, they're not going to be, because I'm taking them home!

GIDEON *comes flying in.*

Come on, let's go.

JULIAN (*off*). We're just trying to honour Sarah's wishes, Gideon.

GIDEON *hands the urn to* MICHELLE.

GIDEON. Hold this, Munchkin.

He dashes out again.

(*Off.*) You people think you know it all and actually, you know horseshit.

ORION (*off*). Gideon, you're no longer an adolescent...

GIDEON (*off*). I'm not afraid to punch either of you.

JULIAN (*off*). Gideon, Gideon, come on.

GIDEON (*off*). Julian, Julian, fuck off.

ANTHONY. I wish he wouldn't shout so much.

MICHELLE. So do I, love. You okay a moment, pet, if I pop out?

ANTHONY. Yeah, I'm fine.

She leaves the urn, goes.

GIDEON (*off*). You're so up yourselves, you don't even know who I am, you never did! Maybe you'd have something to learn.

ANTHONY *perches on the covered table, nervous.*

MICHELLE (*off*). Gideon, you're frightening Anthony...

ANTHONY *picks up the urn. He tries to take the lid off, it's stiff.*

ORION (*off*). I'm going to check on the fire.

GIDEON (*off*). Put it out, we don't want it.

MICHELLE (*off*). Come on, Gideon, they've just got it going.

ORION (*off*). We would like to say goodbye, even if you take the ashes.

The lid pops off, ash spills.

ANTHONY. Oh!

ANTHONY *tries to gather it up. Snatches of argument continue as the others tussle outside.*

ORION, JULIAN, GIDEON *and* MICHELLE (*off*). Come on, be reasonable. – Stop telling me how to live! – Hush, now, Gideon. – Let's just try it and see, shall we? – She liked fires. – Well, I don't. (*Etc.*)

JULIAN *continually tries to make contact with* GIDEON.

JULIAN (*off*). Breathe, just breathe.

GIDEON (*off*). Get your hands off me!

JULIAN (*off*). Can we just agree, Gideon, that your mother was an amazing woman whom we all loved very much.

GIDEON. She lived on scraps of love, dope and sex.

ORION (*off*). Here's to the next stage of her existence.

GIDEON *comes flying in.* ANTHONY *shoves the lid back on.*

GIDEON. Get your jacket, Anthony.

JULIAN *comes in, followed by* MICHELLE *and* ORION, *and then* JESS (*a younger member of the commune*).

JULIAN. How's it going, Anthony?

ANTHONY. Okay.

JESS. I brought a bottle of elderflower over.

JULIAN. Jess, thanks, that's great.

He's tactile with her.

This is Gideon, Sarah's son.

JESS. Hiya.

GIDEON. My wife, Michelle.

JESS. Hello.

GIDEON. My son, Anthony.

JESS. Hello, Anthony, pleased to meet you.

GIDEON. And, my mother, whom I guess you knew, is in the pot.

JESS. I'm so sorry.

Beat. She realises she's forgotten the glasses.

Ooh, I didn't bring glasses...

ORION. I'll get them.

He goes.

JESS. It was a lovely cremation.

GIDEON. Good. Couldn't make it.

JULIAN. No.

JESS. She was a lovely woman, your mum.

GIDEON. Yup.

JESS. Even when her hair fell out, she was so beautiful, still.

GIDEON. Good.

JULIAN. It's a real advantage to this living, if somebody gets sick there are others to cook and care for them.

GIDEON. I couldn't get there, I had a family of my own to look after.

JULIAN. I was just pointing out an up-side of our way of life, you tend to look at the negatives.

GIDEON. That's my experience.

JESS. Wow, it's not mine.

JULIAN. How about you, Michelle, does the communal life appeal to you?

MICHELLE. I don't know much about it, really, but I can imagine it working.

JULIAN. Kids love it here. Lots of people, fresh air.

GIDEON. We live on farmland, so air's not a problem.

JULIAN. Do you have many folk around you?

MICHELLE. No.

GIDEON. Just animals, that's how we like it.

JULIAN. Do you farm the animals?

MICHELLE *and* GIDEON. No.

GIDEON. We're not a meat-eating family.

MICHELLE. Except me.

JULIAN (*to* ANTHONY). Are you vegetarian, Anthony?

ANTHONY. I don't know.

GIDEON. His throat swells up.

MICHELLE. From tomatoes / and citrus fruits.

GIDEON. From meat.

MICHELLE. But he gets anaemic.

GIDEON. So, plenty spinach.

   Silence. To ANTHONY.

JULIAN. Would you like to go outside?

   ORION *comes back with glasses.*

   Some of the kids are out playing with the dogs.

MICHELLE. Go on, if you'd like to.

GIDEON. Don't go far.

   ANTHONY *leaves.* ORION *pours glasses of wine, hands them round.*

MICHELLE. Thank you.

JULIAN. Oh, thank you.

   ORION *raises his glass.*

ORION. To Sarah. She loved you, Gideon.

GIDEON. What do you mean, she loved me? She hardly ever came to see us, never wrote, never called.

MICHELLE. We didn't keep in touch, either.

GIDEON. She probably didn't give a shit, who knows?

JULIAN. / Alright.

MICHELLE. / Not now, Gideon.

GIDEON. I don't know why I'm standing here drinking with you lot. I've no intention of 'sharing'. What about you, Jess, are you 'sharing' with Julian? Three in a bed, was it, with my mother, before she got sick?

JULIAN. Gideon...

GIDEON (*to* MICHELLE). You got the ashes?

MICHELLE. Yes.

GIDEON. Come on then, let's go. Where's Ant?

MICHELLE. I'll fetch him.

She goes.

GIDEON. Actually, I'm taking that cloth.

JULIAN. The cloth?

ORION. Let him take it.

JULIAN. Sure.

GIDEON *pulls the cloth off the table.*

GIDEON. What the... what the fuck?

The stumpy, scrappy table is revealed.

Is this her table?

JULIAN. Hers?

GIDEON. Is this her fucking table, you morons?

JULIAN. That was a gift from your mother –

GIDEON. No –

JULIAN. To the community.

GIDEON. Where are the legs? What's happened to it, you gob-shites?

ORION. It charts our history, that table.

MICHELLE *rushes in with* ANTHONY.

MICHELLE. Gideon, he's been bitten by a dog. (*To the others.*) Do you have antiseptic, or Germolene?

GIDEON. What?

ORION. In the other house.

JULIAN. One of ours?

GIDEON. Game over, we're taking the table and going.

MICHELLE. He needs antiseptic, Gideon.

GIDEON. Get him in the van, Miche', we're leaving, now.

MICHELLE (*quietly to* GIDEON). It's a four-hour drive!

JESS. I have a plaster, if you need one?

GIDEON. Open the doors, start up the engine. Where are the legs, tell me where the fucking legs are or I'll kill you.

ORION. Uh, the candlesticks…

ORION *indicates four charred plinths.* GIDEON *steams round the room, knocking candles off them.*

GIDEON. You godforsaken imbeciles!

MICHELLE. Our son has been bitten by a dog, Gideon, can you please pay attention?

GIDEON. I am, we're leaving.

He dumps the legs in MICHELLE's *arms.*

MICHELLE (*trying desperately to get through to him*). We need to bathe it, he needs antiseptic.

GIDEON. We've got salt at home.

GIDEON *starts dragging the table out*.

Michelle, take the other end, Michelle.

JULIAN. Hey, Gideon, we can help, you know? We're practised in cooperation.

MICHELLE (*to* ORION). / Could you please get us some Germolene?

GIDEON. It's my table, not yours!

JULIAN. There's no reason for us to behave like animals.

JESS (*sneaking out*). / I'll go get the Germolene.

GIDEON. You can talk, you fucking pervert. Don't touch my table, take your hands off it!

GIDEON *drags the table on his back*.

'Chelle!

ORION *and* JULIAN *try to help*. GIDEON *erupts violently*.

Leave us, go on, fuck off, fuck off!

MICHELLE, JULIAN, ORION, ANTHONY. / Dad... – Come on, Gideon. – Please, calm down. – We just want to help, you know? – Dad. – Gideon... (*Etc.*)

GIDEON. Fuck off, fuck off, fuck off, you bunch of swines, go away, go away, fuck off, fuck off, FUCK OFF! (*Etc.*)

JULIAN *and* ORION *recede*. GIDEON *drops the table. It lands, with a bang, upside down*.

MICHELLE. Gideon?

MICHELLE *stops, cries suddenly*.

ANTHONY. You all right, Mum?

MICHELLE. Yeah.

ANTHONY. Mum?

MICHELLE. Yes, pet, I'm sorry. I'm sorry.

> GIDEON *falls away*. ANTHONY *gathers up the legs. He tries to reattach one*. MICHELLE *gets up. One by one, she reattaches the table legs. As she does, all the ancestors gather round*.

ALL (*singing*).
>> Lay me low, lay me low, lay me low
>> Where no one can see me
>> Where no one can find me
>> Where no one can hurt me.

> ANTHONY *helps her to turn it the right way up, then leaves*.

>> Show me the way, help me to say
>> All that I need to
>> All that I needed you gave me
>> All that I wanted you made me
>> When I stumbled you saved me
>> Lay me low...

> *As they sing, the ancestors pass* MICHELLE *all the things she needs to lay the table*.

>> Throw me a line, help me to find
>> Something to cling to
>> When the loneliness haunts me
>> When the bitterness taunts me
>> When the emptiness eats me.
>> Lay me low...

> *The table is set. In London, they're back where they were.*

MICHELLE. How long are you staying, Gideon?

GIDEON. I don't intend to go again.

MICHELLE. Thought not. I'd like to know what your plans are, regarding this family?

GIDEON. We all change, Michelle. I've had a lot of time to go over stuff, find the valves, let some pressure off.

MICHELLE. Pills, was it, in the end?

GIDEON. No. How about you?

MICHELLE. What do you mean?

GIDEON. You seem remarkably happy to be with the family.

MICHELLE. Mm.

GIDEON. And good at it.

MICHELLE. Do I get the Best Grandma Award? I'm not doing it to win.

GIDEON. I didn't mean to offend you.

MICHELLE. It takes a long time to find a life. In my experience, by the time you do, it's nearly over.

GIDEON. So, you have one, then?

MICHELLE. A life?

GIDEON. Anthony tells me you're offered more work than you can manage, designing extensions.

MICHELLE. I'm busy, if that's what you're asking.

GIDEON. Do you have a partner?

MICHELLE. Nothing permanent. What about you, a nice Thai bride?

GIDEON. No, you just weave on through, you know? Plus, it means I've been able to do what I want to do.

MICHELLE. So long as nothing interrupts that.

GIDEON. Ouch.

It costs her huge effort, but MICHELLE *tries to be less brittle.*

MICHELLE. I'm not setting out to offend you, either.

GIDEON. I appreciate I wasn't an easy man to be with, back in the day, and that I was over-defensive for a number of years afterwards.

MICHELLE. Just a few.

GIDEON. I'd like to say, I'm trying to say – sorry.

MICHELLE. Are you?

GIDEON. I'm sorry.

MICHELLE. I don't need your apology. What kind of an excuse is sorry?

GIDEON. I'm not doing it for you, I'm doing it for us.

MICHELLE. There is no us, Gideon. You'd have to work damn hard on manifesting that one.

GIDEON. That's what I intend to do. Because, basically, you've got our son and his family –

MICHELLE. Got them? I haven't got them. I haven't *got* anyone. Anthony and Ben have got each other, they have Su-Lin, for a few more years… no, Gideon, I am a satellite, I exist in their orbit, and you have no clue how hard I've worked at that.

GIDEON. I can see, and I suppose that I've –

MICHELLE. Come back because you want a bit of what I've put thirty humbling years in to having? Whilst I've cut my life around steering Anthony through, making things okay for him, his partner, his daughter, you think you can just waltz in and snatch yourself that, do you, Gideon? Took a fancy to being a granddad, spotted the cherry on the cake, so you come bouncing home, throw your beam of light – hallelujah, Gideon's back, dedicated family man.

GIDEON. You're laughing at me, 'Chelle, but that's what I always wanted.

MICHELLE. Fat way of showing it, dumping us for all those years.

GIDEON. You asked me to leave.

MICHELLE. I said let's take a break.

GIDEON. You didn't want me, 'Chelle.

MICHELLE. Whoever told you Anthony didn't?

GIDEON. I'm sorry.

MICHELLE. What does it even mean? It's so easy for you to come here now and say that. Saying 'sorry' just doesn't cut it, I've been sorry for years and years. What are you sorry for, Gideon?

GIDEON. You know for what, you've said it, not being here, what should I be sorry for?

MICHELLE. Leaving the country without even telling us, for starters? Calling at Christmas and singing some stupid song you'd just learnt from wherever the hell you were? Posting letters without enough stamps on, which turn up six months late? I can't believe I'm dragging this stuff up.

GIDEON. Sorry.

MICHELLE. Sorry for what? You've got no idea, because you never bothered asking.

Beat.

GIDEON. I'm asking now.

MICHELLE. What do you want, the highlights? A round-up of top moments to be sorry you couldn't be there for?

GIDEON. No, I just mean –

MICHELLE. What about Anthony, age ten, calmly telling me he'd had enough of life and wanted to make the world stop, what did I think was the best way? Anthony, age thirteen, getting swept out on his lilo in Wales and me panicking in my head about how to get hold of you to tell you we'd lost him. His traumas before stepping out the house on any given day of any given year – I'm too stupid, I'm not good enough, I'll never achieve anything. His first relationship. His second relationship – this time with a boy. His first job. Getting the sack from that job for mumbling. The deep insecurity which has dogged Anthony his whole life long, basically, Gideon, coupled with wanting the moon. You paved the way for it, branded it for ever, then missed it, missed it all.

GIDEON. I'd assumed you were better off without me. I didn't feel very lovable.

MICHELLE. That's a very indulgent position for a parent to take.

GIDEON. Everything I do, I do wholeheartedly and you'd asked me to go.

MICHELLE. I had no idea we'd never speak about it again!

Beat.

GIDEON. I didn't expect you to still be so angry, if I'm honest. I'm not saying… I do understand.

MICHELLE. Oh, that's okay then, it's all right if I feel angry because martyr Gideon says so.

GIDEON. I just meant, you're right, of course you're right, we've never gone over it, I don't mind, I can take it.

MICHELLE. I don't care if you can take it or not, frankly, Gideon, because *I* mind, I mind feeling like this all these years on, I do, and no, it's not all right. This hatefulness makes me sick. I'm back there on that stupid farm with nobody to talk to except a constantly sick child, and you manic in the fields erecting barbed-wire fences. This had gone, Gideon, all this was buried and it took me years. I've worked so bloody hard to keep this show on the road – work, family, pets, friends, house, nutrition, meditation, exercise, be patient, have faith, skirt depression, laugh, feel like it makes sense, like you've got a life, and then *you* land slap bang in the middle again after so long, *giving me permission to be angry*. I've got backlogs of your shit stacked up in here and I don't want any of it. I don't want you here, I don't want you round Su-Lin, I don't want you near Anthony, I don't want you infecting this house with your Gideon-ness.

GIDEON. Do you want me to leave?

MICHELLE. Your self-consumed, overbearing…

GIDEON. Shall I leave?

MICHELLE. I'll leave. It's not my place to send you from this house, it's actually not my place, I pop in, do my bit, it works, though, Gideon, it works. That child is so happy and lucky, Ben and Anthony worship every atom of her, and you, you could just…

She does a vice-like motion.

Because that's what you do, crush things.

He starts to go.

GIDEON. I'll leave, Michelle.

MICHELLE. Do what you want, you always did, you always have.

He turns back.

GIDEON. Fuck. Is that what you really think, that I do what I want? If I'd done what I wanted at the time our family separated, I'd have come back and killed you, Michelle, over and over again. Because that was what I passionately wanted, that was the vision that haunted me on my travels – extinguishing you and rescuing Anthony. Kidnapping him, making myself the adventure he'd always longed for. I wanted Anthony, but I didn't get him. I'd put everything I was in to both of you, so I wanted to annihilate you for many years. Every slight I'd ever felt, every obsessive thought rolled into one – you got. I'm not saying it was right, I'm just telling you what I wanted to do, but didn't, and it wasn't what I wanted to be feeling either. When I did pick up a telephone, my heart was clenched so tightly with self-defence, because I knew you'd answer and I couldn't bear to hear you so phoning became a problem. I'm sorry about the stamps, I didn't know about the shortfall. There's lots I don't know, clearly. But if you honestly imagine I go around doing what I want to do, you couldn't be further from the truth. I still get those urges to kick out, to shout and destroy. Coming here, seeing you, half of me wanted to pour petrol on your head and set you alight, the other half wanted to take you. I want to cry, right now, but I'm not. I want to pick that forty-year-old man up and cradle him in my arms like he was still one. I live with these desires all the time, we all do, but I don't act on them, not any more. I've learnt that what I really want is to be even a portion of the man I would die a tiny bit proud of being. At least not die ashamed. I want to clear the hair from off your face because it's fallen in a way that feels familiar to me, but you're a different woman to the one I knew and I wouldn't dream of intruding on a stranger to move the hair off her face.

MICHELLE. It's too late, Gideon.

GIDEON. Not for me, in fairness. Or for Su-Lin. Perhaps not even for Anthony. Isn't it better to have a dad late in life than not at all? I know I've made a mess.

MICHELLE (*not unkindly*). Always back to you, isn't it?

GIDEON. I didn't know how to come home, and you weren't asking...

MICHELLE. You proud fuck. We didn't even know where you were.

GIDEON. I was building houses. For other families to live in.

Beat.

I'm sorry I treated you and Anthony as if you were some kind of cathedral.

ANTHONY *comes in with a tray.*

ANTHONY. Coffee...

GIDEON. Michelle, I've not come here with expectations or demands... All I've come back with is hope, that's it. I'm cradling a small piece of hope that there might be a place for me somewhere in the orbit of my once-upon-a-time family.

MICHELLE. I'm glad you're more settled, I am, and I might be prepared to give you an inch as a result. But if you try and spin that into a mile before you've properly stepped through the door, then forget it. Because despite losing it now and again, I'm more settled too, and I won't put up with any pig-headed shit you come up with from your extra-special, mono-focus Best-family brain, okay?

GIDEON. Okay.

They reach a truce.

MICHELLE. Okay.

(*To* ANTHONY.) I'd like to go home now.

ANTHONY. What, right this minute?

MICHELLE. Yeah, I need to get back. I'll do my share of the washing up and then, if you don't mind, could you possibly give me a lift, please?

ANTHONY. Of course.

MICHELLE. Thank you, love. (*To* GIDEON.) See you, Gid.

She takes plates off.

ANTHONY. Sorry, Dad, I'll just...

GIDEON. No problem, son.

ANTHONY. Ah, Ben won't be home 'til –

GIDEON. Don't worry, whenever.

ANTHONY. Any minute, in fact. Are you happy to hold the fort –?

GIDEON. Of course I'm happy, you do what you have to do.

ANTHONY *goes.* GIDEON, *alone with the table, stretches his arms along it in an embrace. He starts singing softly to himself.*

(*Singing.*)
　　Oh don't be unkind to a duck,
　　For a duck may be somebody's brother,
　　They always live in the swamp
　　Where the weather is always domp...

SU-LIN *comes in.*

SU-LIN. I hate this table, or should I not say that?

GIDEON. It's yours, you can say what you like.

SU-LIN. It's not mine.

GIDEON. It will be.

SU-LIN. I don't want it. I'm going to buy a big glass one from Ikea.

GIDEON. What'll you do with this?

SU-LIN. Freecycle? It's mank.

GIDEON. Why?

SU-LIN. Look at it, it's all cacked-up.

GIDEON. What's cacked it up, though?

SU-LIN. What do you mean?

GIDEON. Pick a cack-up, any cack-up.

SU-LIN. What?

GIDEON. Want to see a coffin scratch?

SU-LIN. Is that the big one?

She points to DAVID*'s gouge.*

GIDEON. It's not, no, nobody knows how that one happened.

SU-LIN. That one, then?

He shakes his head.

GIDEON. Leopard claws.

SU-LIN. Not true.

GIDEON. True.

SU-LIN. What's that from?

GIDEON. Mad nun's nails.

SU-LIN. That pale bit?

GIDEON. Bleach. Or possibly urine.

SU-LIN. Urgh.

She draws a little closer, picks a new patch.

That?

GIDEON. Heartburn.

SU-LIN. Those?

GIDEON. That's a thump and that's a joke gone wrong.

SU-LIN. That?

GIDEON. Bits of flour from five thousand loaves of bread.

SU-LIN. That?

GIDEON. What, the sparkly bits?

SU-LIN. Which sparkly bits?

She looks.

GIDEON. Tiny shards from twenty-seven million boring conversations.

SU-LIN. This?

GIDEON. Prayers.

SU-LIN. Prayers?

He looks at a dot.

GIDEON. Is that nail varnish?

SU-LIN. I spilt Gran's bottle.

GIDEON. Blue? You've made your mark.

SU-LIN. When you went to Africa to see your dad, what was he like?

GIDEON *drops down, goes under the table.*

What?

GIDEON. I didn't say anything.

SU-LIN. Why?

GIDEON. Some things are difficult to say.

SU-LIN. I won't look.

GIDEON. How does that help?

SU-LIN. I don't know. Go on, you can tell me now.

GIDEON (*from under the table*). I never met him.

SU-LIN. You said you did!

GIDEON. I went to his grave. He died before I got there. Would you like to see his writing?

SU-LIN. Go on then.

GIDEON *shows her.*

'Amor Patris, J.H.' What does 'Amor Patris' mean?

Under the table, GIDEON *is in the same position he was in at the start. He's crying.*

GIDEON. Love of the Father.

SU-LIN *hears him cry. She's still on the table. Eventually, she knocks on it – knock knock. No response. Knock knock again.*

Who's there?

SU-LIN. Boo.

Getting the joke.

GIDEON. Boo hoo.

SU-LIN. Sing something else.

GIDEON (*singing*).
    Dear Lord and Father of mankind
    Forgive our foolish ways –

SU-LIN (*interrupting*). Boring.

GIDEON (*singing*).
    Napolo-Polo
    Napidemu-Deh
    Pollo-Pollo, poo!

SU-LIN. Childish.

GIDEON (*singing*).
>   *Yu go-ngo gum sung tzu din hai…*

SU-LIN. Doesn't go like that.

GIDEON. Go on then.

SU-LIN (*singing*).
>   *Yu go-ngo gum sung tzu din hai ya go yen*
>   *Mo soh why men ya ngo hay tzoy wa sing…*

GIDEON *joins in. They belt it out together, him from under the table, her on top.*

SU-LIN *and* GIDEON (*singing*).
>   *U go mo yam zan tzoy foo gno sang woh see*
>   *Ho bi tzoi mun soy hey gno.*

The ancestors join in.

ALL (*singing*).
>   *Yu go-ngo gum sung tzu din hai ya go yen,*
>   *Mo soh why men ya ngo hay tzoy wa sing,*
>   *U go mo yam zan tzoy foo gno sang woh see*
>   *Ho bi tzoi mun soy hey gno.*

DAVID *comes in and gives the table one last check with his fingers.*

The End.

www.nickhernbooks.co.uk

facebook.com/nickhernbooks

twitter.com/nickhernbooks